RealitySpirituality

The Truth About Happiness

Rebecca L. Norrington

REALITYSPIRITUALITY: *The Truth About Happiness*
Rebecca L. Norrington
Mother—Daughter—SoulMate—Intuitive—
Healer—Mystic—Teacher

Copyright © 2014 by Rebecca L. Norrington
All rights reserved.

No part of this publication may be reproduced, stored in a retrieval system, or transmitted in any form or by any means electronic, mechanical, photocopying, recording, or otherwise, without the written permission of the author or publisher.

ISBN: 978-1-304-84701-0

Publisher: Lulu Press, Inc.
Quantities printed in USA by 48HrBooks (www.48HrBooks.com)
Editor: Joyce Shafer (http://editmybookandmore.weebly.com)
Cover Design: Kristin Chase Klaiber (kristymcqueen@yahoo.com)
Interior Book Design: Integrative Ink (www.integrativeink.com)
Cover Photos: Shannon M. West (www.smwimages.com)

DEDICATION

In Loving Memory of my father—Ralph Norrington. He'd often tell me, "This is a great life," but I never believed him ... until now.

To Marcelle D. Norrington, who chose me to be her only daughter. Our relationship evolves every day. I love you, Mommy.

To my only son—Nathan M. Norrington. You are the reason I needed to find answers.

To Ccid E. Cartwright, my Soul- and Best-Mate. I would not be me without you. I love you and your family.

To everyone else, whether you know it or believe it, you've all made a huge contribution to my spiritual growth ... and I am grateful.

TABLE OF CONTENTS

ACKNOWLEDGMENTS xi

PREFACE 1
    In the Beginning—The Girl Without a Name 1
    Back Story 2
    The Secret 4

INTRODUCTION 7
    My Search 8
    What Is RealitySpirituality? 9

CHAPTER 1 13
    Happiness Is More Than a Feeling 13
    You Have to Want to Be Happy More than You Want Anything Else 15
    When You Make Happiness a Priority 17
    Living Unconsciously—Your Obstacle to Happiness 19
    Practice, Practice, Practice 22
    Happiness versus Suffering, the Choice Is Yours 22
    Who Defines Suffering—Man or God? 23
    Do You Know Who You Are? 24

CHAPTER 2 27
    Universe versus Man 27
    The Pope and the Serial Killer 28
    Realms of the Universe 30

The Realm of Knowing 31
The Realm of Thinking.. 31
What Is Real and What Is an Illusion?.. 33

CHAPTER 3 37
Everything Is Energy 37
The Importance of Understanding the Laws of the Universe.. 38
The Laws of the Universe 39
Immutable and Mutable Laws 39
   1. The Law of Mentalism (Immutable) 40
   2. The Law of Correspondence (Immutable) 40
   3. The Law of Vibration (Immutable) 41
   Your Personal Vibration 41
   4. The Law of Polarity (Mutable) 43
   5. The Law of Rhythm (Mutable) 44
   6. The Law of Cause and Effect (Mutable) 45
   7. The Law of Gender (Mutable) 46
The Law of Attraction Is Part of the Equation 46
The Mental Laws 47
The Importance of Understanding Mental Laws................... 47
What is a Law? 47
   1. The Law Of Thoughts Arising 49
   2. The Law Of Witnessing 49
   3. The Law Of Naming.. 50
   4. The Law Of Cause And Effect 50
   5. The Law Of Emotion 51
   6. The Law Of Focus.. 51
   7. The Law Of Free Will.. 52
   8. The Law Of Underlying Beliefs 53
   9. The Law Of Substitution 53
   10. The Law Of Mental Equivalents 53
   11. The Mental Law Of Truth 54

CHAPTER 4 55
The Purpose of Life... 55
The Meaning of Life 55
What's So Important?... 56

CHAPTER 5 59
Happiness: Mission Possible—
Only if You're Willing to Lose Control 59
Trying to Control Anything or Anyone Leads to Unhappiness .. 61
Mastering Self—My Greatest Accomplishment 62
Elements of Self-Mastery 66
Your Opinion Is My Opinion—Peace & Happiness at All Costs.... 66
How Does the Law of Relationship Harmony Work? 68
What's Your Opinion? 69
My Past Exposed 70
Guilty or Not Guilty 71
What's My Opinion? 73
Democrats versus Republicans, and Happiness 74
I Relapsed 78
A Dose of Irritation 80
Here Comes Da Judge 81
Universe to the Rescue 81

CHAPTER 6 85
Happiness and Forgiveness 85
Death and Forgiveness 87
Twenty Years Later 88
Hurry Up, Mom 90
Forgive as Quickly as Possible 91
How to Forgive Instantly 92
When You Are Challenged 93
Forgive Yourself 94

CHAPTER 7 97
Death and Happiness 97
Back Story 98
My History 100

    Ask and It Is Given 101
    Ralph Norrington, My Father 102
    What Pancake Taught Me 113
    Back Story 114
    Lessons 117

CHAPTER 8 123
    How to Live in the Moment 123
    Programmed at Birth 124
    Are Our Thoughts the Enemy? 124
    What's so Great about Living in the Moment? 126

CHAPTER 9 127
    The Bitter Pill of Dissatisfaction 127
    Can Satisfaction Be Guaranteed? 129

CHAPTER 10 133
    Money and Happiness 133
    Background 134
    Money = Success? 136
    My Money Chakra Is Blocked 136
    What I Thought about Money Was the Problem 137
    A New Perspective 138

CHAPTER 11 141
    Holidays and Happiness 141
    Back Story 142
    Is It Possible to Be Single and Happy on Valentine's Day? 144
    What Are You Doing for the Holidays? 146
    My New Year's Resolution for 2014 147

CHAPTER 12 151
    Be the Change You Want to See in the World 151
    The Solution 155

360 Ways to Be Happy 156
I Am at Peace 157
Universe, What Did You Say? 158
Universe, Why? 160

CHAPTER 13 163
Ask Rebecca Anything! 163
How to Relieve Anxiety While in the Moment 166
Your Worrying Has Got to Stop 171
Hear Ye, Hear Ye—I'm Worried about You 172
The Truth about Worrying 173
The Truth about the Ego 178
What We Resist Persists and What We Focus on Grows 180
How I Interact with My Ego 180
Change Your Perspective 180
Who Am I? 182
Quiet as a Mouse 184
360 Choices to Happiness 186
Intention and Commitment 187
Your Husband and Making Marriage Work 188
Gratitude 190
Another Perspective 190
University of Happiness Attendance Guidelines 198
What Else Is Wrong? 202
Happiness Is Always My Priority 203
A Few Characteristics of Happy People 204
Finally 205
RealitySpirituality Radio Show—January 2014 206
RealitySpirituality Radio Show—February 15, 2014 208

CHAPTER 14 211
REBECCA L. NORRINGTON QUOTES 211

CHAPTER 15 223
    Conclusion: Life Is a Gift 223

ABOUT THE AUTHOR 225
    Authors That Changed My Life 227
    Family 228

AUTHOR'S NOTE 229

ACKNOWLEDGMENTS

I've been writing this book for over fifteen years. One of the many lessons I've learned is that I cannot speed up, slow down, or stop what the Universe has planned for me. I've finally surrendered and accepted my destiny. Universe, thank you for choosing me to write this book.

Foremost, I'd like to thank Ccid, my spiritual partner in this life. The Universe had plans for us greater than our own. I'll never forget the first time you looked into my eyes and said, "All I see is drama." I was raising my only child, and I knew then that I had to make a change. Thank you for sharing that Truth with me, and thank you for loving my son as though he's your own.

Nathan, my only son, I love you regardless of what you do and regardless of what you don't do.

Steve-O, my ex-husband, after years of challenges, you've managed to remain a friend. I love you.

Joyce Shafer, my spiritual mother, sister, and friend. I remember the first time we spoke: I shared with you endless amounts of negative judgments and thoughts about myself.

Still, you loved me, accepted me, and encouraged me with Universal patience to find another way to live. Thank you for being an important part of my journey of discovery and growth. I love you, JLS.

Juanita, Romie, Donna—my girlfriends—you don't know the meaning of obligation or guilt. You have always loved me unconditionally, and I am truly grateful for our friendship. I love you all.

To the thousands of students I've taught at "the gym" over thirty-plus years, thank you for being my favorite *audience*.

Ernest Holmes, visionary and spiritual teacher—your books, *Science of Mind* and *Living the Science of Mind* are my foundation. I am truly grateful for the needed guidance. Thank you for helping me to change the direction of my life.

To Abraham, and Jerry and Esther Hicks—I'm grateful for your message. Abraham, your words say it all: "You cannot have a happy ending to an unhappy journey." I AM never complete.

To Barbara Berger and Tim Ray—for granting permission to include The Mental Laws published in their book, *The Awakening Human Being – A Guide to the Power of Mind.*

The Seven Universal Laws segment was obtained, in part, from an article by Tania Kotsos, posted on her Website, Mind Your Reality, which she obtained from *The Science of Being* and *The Kybalion*.

The following segments were previously published, in part, in my co-authored book, *If I Knew Then What I Know Now, Our Quest for Quality or Life*: Happiness and Forgiveness,

RealitySpirituality: The Truth About Happiness

Forgive as Quickly as Possible, How to Forgive Instantly, Five Facts about Forgiveness, When You are Challenged, and Life is a Gift.

PREFACE

In the Beginning—The Girl Without a Name

Because of the progress in race relations we experience today, it's hard for some in younger age groups to imagine the racial climate in the United States in 1955. That year, as in prior decades, race relations between blacks and whites were, at best, strained and, at worst, extremely volatile. Two significant events happened on December 1, 1955: on a crowded bus in Montgomery, Alabama, Rosa Parks refused to obey a bus driver's command to give up her seat for a white passenger, an action which sparked the famous Montgomery Bus Boycott that eventually led to the modern Civil Rights Movement; and, a little girl without a name was born on a cold, damp winter day in Los Angeles, California.

The little girl was one of nine babies delivered that day by a third-year medical student at Los Angeles County Hospital, also known simply as "County," where the city's underprivileged and minorities began their lives. Delivery of the baby was quick and easy, with no complications. The newborn was Addie Williams' fifth of six children she would eventually bear.

Addie gazed at her baby girl's tiny frame and face, void of feeling overjoyed about her new arrival or of feeling any maternal instincts for her daughter. Instead, she was consumed with shame, guilt, and embarrassment. It was as though she'd just been caught for an unthinkable crime and was now sentenced to a life in prison.

Back Story

Addie was a young, beautiful, troubled, and uneducated black woman. At sixteen, she found herself pregnant and forced to marry Ed Williams, a kind young black man she would eventually disrespect with each passing year. Before the birth of this baby girl, Addie and Ed raised four children. Addie's baby born on December 1, 1955, was the result of an "unholy" union, a "business" proposition, so to speak.

Howard Solomon was the owner of the garment factory where Addie worked. He was a white man, with a wife and children of his own, and he paid Addie to have sex with him. It was a mutual arrangement that went on for several months before she got pregnant. When Addie told Howard she was pregnant, he gave her $400 and a command to "get rid of it." Instead of using the money for an abortion, Addie purchased a car and found another job. Knowing there was a fifty-fifty chance the child could belong to her husband, she kept this secret for nine months, until the baby girl was born. Now, her nine-month bi-racial secret was out, literally and figuratively, staring her in the face. Addie was sick with panic.

At first glance, Ed Williams knew the newborn wasn't his. The baby's complexion was fair, almost white. This wasn't the first time Addie had broken her vows. This time she had crossed all boundaries of decency and forgiveness by having an affair with a white man. Feeling humiliated and betrayed an angry Ed threatencd Addie with divorce, before leaving her hospital room.

I can only speculate about the thoughts that tormented Addie on that day. In reality, her life and her stability were crumbling with every moment of this baby's existence. The child's presence alone would initiate a lifetime of stares, questions, and explanations. Her family was being threatened, threatened by an innocent baby without a name. Admittedly, she'd gotten herself into this mess and she was determined to get herself out of it: Addie had no one to blame but herself. One of Addie's best traits was being a survivor. After a couple of days, she contrived a solution to her problem because there was no way in hell she was going to allow this tiny creature to ruin her life. The nameless baby had to disappear, had to literally vanish from the face of the Earth—or at least from her life. But how?

Addie decided to put the baby up for adoption. Her husband agreed. However, it wasn't going to be that simple. For nine months Addie had publically carried this baby in full sight. All of Addie's relatives, both in and out of state, knew she was pregnant. How was a newborn baby going to disappear without an explanation? Two weeks after the child's birth, the solution came to mind.

The Secret

It was another cold, damp afternoon, much like the day of the child's birth, when Addie and Ed packed up all of the newborn's belongings. It was amazing how much had been accumulated during the pregnancy. The crib, clothes, bottles, and several toys were quickly packed and hauled out of the house during one predestined afternoon, while Addie's four other children attended school. It was exactly two weeks after her birth when the baby girl without a name left her first home.

Jackie Williams was Addie's oldest daughter. She was sixteen years old at the time of her baby sister's birth. Jackie had been excited about the arrival of the newest member of the family. She developed a daily routine of running home from high school to care for her newborn sister, and Addie was always grateful for the break. However, this particular day was different.

Addie looked away as Jackie rushed in, dropped her books on the kitchen table, and skipped toward the bedroom she'd been sharing with her new sister. When Jackie reached the bedroom door, she stopped momentarily. Something was odd. Jackie's expression froze and she went into shock as she stepped into the emptied room. Jackie's bed was still there, but her baby sister's crib was gone! The bottles that were kept on the dresser were gone! The small toys stacked in the corner of the room, given as gifts months before her sister's birth, were gone. The closet door was open to expose several empty shelves. Her new baby sister was gone! It looked as though the baby had never existed. Jackie screamed to her Mother, "What happened to my sister? Where's my sister?"

Jackie ran into the kitchen were Addie was sitting quietly at the table, unaffected by her daughter's hysterical screams. "That baby died this morning," she calmly told her oldest daughter. Addie repeated the lie to her three other children. She repeated the lie to her sisters, brothers, aunts, uncles, friends, grocery store clerks, bank tellers, co-workers, and neighbors. Only she and Ed knew the truth. Miraculously, they kept the secret for over forty years.

In 1996, on a blistering hot summer day in August, the "dead" nameless baby girl resurfaced in their lives. This was the story of my beginning.

To be continued...
Rebecca L. Norrington

INTRODUCTION

I've wanted to write a book for over fifteen years. One of the many lessons I've learned is that I cannot speed up or slow down or stop what the Universe has planned for me. I know that everything that happens to me happens at precisely the right moment. And, in fact, that's how this book finally manifested.

As far back as I can remember, I've consistently asked the Universe for two things: to live to my potential and to be happy.

I've been blessed with parents who actually chose me to support. I have a son who is amazing. I've been blessed with material things. I've been blessed with good health. I've been blessed to travel to several breathtaking destinations. I've attained more than a few titles and experiences. I've been blessed with an endless number of personal relationships. Yes, from the outside looking in, you would think I had it all. However, the truth is that despite all the blessings mentioned, I was missing one essential ingredient—happiness. To be clear, the happiness I'm referring to is an unwavering state of internal peace. It was easy to be happy and at peace when things were going great, but I lost it whenever I was challenged and life *went south*.

Further, what I thought would "make" me happy never lasted. I had been very happy during countless moments in my life, but I wanted more, much more. I wanted to be happy all the time. Was that even possible? I was determined to find out.

My Search

At first I thought I wasn't happy because I didn't have a purpose. I actually spent decades searching for my "unique purpose." Why was I here? What am I supposed to be doing with my life? What gift(s) did I have to share with the world? What am I passionate about? I just knew that when I discovered the answers to those questions, I would be happy. Wrong again.

I discovered that the happiness I sought could only be accessed from within. There are no exceptions to this rule—happiness comes from within, and this is true for each of us. It's been decades of searching, discovering, and experimenting, for me to finally find out HOW to remain happy—regardless of any external circumstances. This knowledge has transformed my personal life and the immediate world around me, as well.

My intention, in this book, is to share with you everything I've learned, so far, about how to sustain happiness. First, know that remaining happy in every waking moment *is* possible. Second, know that all you have to do is make being happy your number-one priority and then commit to the goal. Finally, I am here to support you through your journey of discovering heaven on Earth.

What Is RealitySpirituality?

Close your eyes and remember a time when you experienced an indescribable moment… A moment that connected you with the Energy that creates worlds … An unforgettable moment that you felt the power of Creation, Itself … A moment when you were connected with Heaven and Earth. You were overwhelmed with emotion. Every cell in your body was in harmony with all God's creatures, nature—everything in existence. You were happy and at peace. You were overcome with gratitude for the experience you were having. Your feelings were intense and perhaps you cried uncontrollably with joy. Are you able to remember a moment or several moments like that? Can you remember how that moment felt—now, today, at this moment? Do you believe that you can feel that good for the majority of this life? I do. And RealitySpirituality teaches you how it can be possible for you, too.

RealitySpirituality is not a religion. It is guidance that can assist you to be and live connected to *the* most powerful Energy Source. What is our most powerful Energy Source? People use one of the following names or terms for it: God, Buddha, Higher Power, Source Energy, Source, Spirit, and so forth. RealitySpirituality uses the term Universe.

RealitySpirituality focuses on common, everyday life experiences and the connection between our daily experiences and spirituality. It dissects everyday life experiences down to the least common denominator, to reveal why we're not as happy as we could be.

RealitySpirituality teaches us the importance of our personal vibration and that our personal vibration determines to what degree and how often we will experience happiness.

RealitySpirituality focuses on the journey and how to create and experience the happiest journey imaginable. It believes "happily ever after" is possible. When RealitySpirituality uses the word *happy*, it refers to an internal happiness; an unwavering peace of mind; an internal contentment; a knowing that everything that happens is happening for a Divine reason; that everything in this world is unfolding exactly the way it's supposed to.

RealitySpirituality teaches a *knowing* that your life, my life, and everyone's life is in perfect order. Not only is everything in perfect order, but every experience and every circumstance is *ultimately* a gift: the Universe does not make mistakes.

RealitySpirituality teaches that we do not have control over what happens to us, but we do have control over our perspectives, our responses, our behaviors, our words, our vibration, and our attitude. Our personal vibration determines how we respond to people and circumstances. Our responses to our daily experiences determine what type of journey we are going to experience. RealitySpirituality focuses closely on our personal vibration and teaches us how to shift our personal vibration in an instant.

RealitySpirituality teaches that your relationship with the Universe is going to be different than my relationship with the Universe. Why? Because we are all as different as our fingerprints. Each and every one of us is gloriously unique. And our relationship to the Universe is just as unique and personal.

RealitySpirituality does not claim to have all the answers. However, it does have answers that have been revealed in my life, as my experiences—and I'm sharing them with you so you can benefit, as well. It's the format in which I share my personal challenges, lessons, and evolution throughout three decades. I also use it to share a wide range of perspectives, unique strategies, and behaviors that promise to add to your happiness, regardless of your circumstances.

RealitySpirituality teaches us that we all have a choice. We all have the free will to decide whether or not we want to be happy or unhappy.

RealitySpirituality also believes that our emotions are our choice, as well. The concept that our emotions are a choice is revolutionary in nature. However, RealitySpirituality can *prove* that our emotions are a choice we make in every moment. And as our emotions are a choice, why would anyone choose to be sad, angry, frustrated, irritated, or annoyed? It teaches which emotions and behaviors subtract from happiness and which emotions and behaviors add to happiness. It does not believe circumstances, events, or even other people contribute to a person's emotions. It teaches how to eliminate (if you choose to) emotions that are manmade.

RealitySpirituality teaches us to eliminate all labels. It teaches us what the definition of *real* power is. It teaches us the importance of our personal vibration. And it focuses on sharing what's really important in this life.

RealitySpirituality teaches how to stay and live connected to the Universe. It teaches the difference between the Universal Voice and the manmade voice.

RealitySpirituality teaches how to maintain internal freedom. It teaches which words to eliminate from your vocabulary, if you want to be happier.

RealitySpirituality teaches how to live in the present moment.

RealitySpirituality teaches how to focus on what's right instead of focusing on what's wrong.

RealitySpirituality teaches that everything in our outer world is a reflection of our inner world. It encourages us to commit to looking in the mirror for all of the answers.

And, finally, RealitySpirituality uses Universal Laws, along with the wisdom of Ernest Holmes, Abraham-Hicks, and the Voice of the Universe as a foundation for all of its teachings.

CHAPTER 1

Happiness Is More Than a Feeling

Happiness comes from within. There are no exceptions to this rule.
~rln

I didn't always want to be happy. How do I know this? Because I eventually realized I lived an unconscious life. I lived my life reacting to people and circumstances. Yes, I was programmed to behave and respond (or react) just as most people are. I'd also been brainwashed to feel bad if my external circumstances fell short of my expectations. I now recognize that my learned behavior wasn't my fault, but it *was* a result of not knowing another way to live—until now.

See if any of this sounds familiar?

If someone slighted me, I got angry. Guess what? You can't be happy and angry at the same.

If I didn't have enough money in the bank, I worried. Guess what? You can't be happy and worried at the same time.

If I lost a job or didn't get the job, I was disappointed. Guess what? You can't be disappointed and happy at the same time.

If I didn't have enough achievements or titles behind my name, I was dissatisfied. Guess what? You can't feel dissatisfied and grateful (and happy) at the same time.

I've learned after decades of searching for answers that I have a choice as to how I want to feel. This is an important and necessary concept to digest: I have a choice as to how I want to feel—and so do you. Who knew?! In every waking moment, we exercise choices, either consciously or subconsciously. Yes, when you stop to think about it, in every moment, we're choosing between the following emotional behaviors.

Peace or Drama
Acceptance or Judgment
Flowing or Resisting
Love or Fear

What I've discovered is that being happy is a moment-by-moment conscious decision.

I spent the majority of my life being unhappy, and I was tired of that feeling. But, was it possible to feel happy all the time? That question led me to decades of study, experience, and personal evolution. Let me share with you that it is possible to sustain happiness, regardless of any external circumstances. This truth has changed my life, and now I want to share with you everything I've learned—so far.

My intention for writing this book is to offer you insights on how to make different choices—that is, better choices that pertain to types of behavior, unique strategies, and an endless array of perspectives that will aid you, my dear reader, to become more aware of your day-to-day choices.

You Have to Want to Be Happy More than You Want Anything Else

Imagine you live alone. It's a relatively crime-free neighborhood. Your sense of security is justified. You have always felt safe in your home, and there's never been a reason not to ... until tonight. It's 2:00 A.M. You're sound asleep, unaware of the harrowing danger you're about to face.

Quietly and purposely, a stranger enters your home through a back window you keep ajar. You're a sound sleeper, so you don't hear the window being forced more open or the footsteps walking throughout your home. The stranger, holding a flashlight, methodically searches each room, collecting your valuable items in a black over-sized garbage bag. The stranger eventually arrives at your bedroom door. Silently, he enters your room.

Like most of us, the bedroom is where you keep your most valuable possessions. Your jewelry is located in an ornate jewelry box on a nightstand next to your bed. The stranger rifles through your jewelry, grabbing everything. Your sixth sense is awakened by an indescribable unrest. Your eyes open slowly, while still unsure why. The stranger notices you awakening. This story is not going to have a happy ending. When you realize you're not alone, you begin to panic. The stranger also panics, and he instantly realizes he has a problem. YOU have become the stranger's problem.

You're flooded with emotions of shock and terror. Your voice fails you as you attempt to scream. Instinctively, the intruder snatches the pillow from behind your head and begins to use it as a deadly weapon. He covers your face with the pillow. You're unable to stop him. Instinctively, you struggle to grab his arms in an attempt save yourself. You're strong, but he's stronger, much stronger. In a futile attempt to attack, you hit him with both fists. Unfortunately for you, his hold on the pillow does not budge.

The more you struggle, the weaker you become. Panic begins to set in because now you're literally struggling to breathe. You're fighting for your life while you're fighting for breath. Without the ability to breathe, you'll die. Your ONLY focus is survival. Yes or yes? Okay, take a breath. The story is over and you're safe!

What the hell is my point?! What a great question; and I'm glad you asked. My point is this: you have to commit to wanting to be happy with the same amount of energy and fervor that you *want to breathe!*

I remember sharing this same story with a close relative. He was experiencing challenging moments in his life, and asked for my counsel. When I finished the hypothetical story I just shared, my relative looked directly into my eyes and said, "I guess I don't want to be happy that bad." I had a quizzical look on my face because I thought I hadn't heard him correctly. He repeated his statement loud and clear: "I don't want to be happy that bad."

Since that moment, I've discovered that happiness is NOT a PRIORITY for a lot of people, and that's okay . . . for them. Remember the lyrics from "Everyday People" sung by Sly and the Family Stone: "And different stokes for different folks, and so on and so on and scooby dooby doo-bee"? However, let me tell you that when I made the commitment to make happiness my priority, my life changed. The change is evident in every moment of my day. And the change is evident is every single relationship I'm in, whether that's family, friends, co-workers, or strangers on the street. No delayed gratification here. Now, if YOU are interested in prioritizing happiness in your life, there are a few *ground rules* you must follow.

- Your happiness is your responsibility.
- Your thoughts and your behaviors must change.
- Blaming anyone or any circumstance for your unhappiness is not allowed.

When You Make Happiness a Priority

- You will mentally and emotionally begin to RELAX.
- You will begin to TRUST and KNOW that everything that happens "to" you is in Divine order. It's ALL happening for your BETTERMENT.
- You will begin to experience even MORE happiness.

- TOXIC emotions (emotions that subtract from happiness) such as anger, irritation, fear, sadness, resentment, jealously, rage, loneliness, hatred, shame, blame, hostility, anxiety, despair, hopelessness, impatience, negativity—the list is endless—will begin to LOSE their power and eventually cease to exist in your life! Sounds too good to be true? It is true, and I'm proof.
- Toxic emotions will be replaced with emotions that will feed your soul. You will begin to feel more gratitude, joy, contentment, inner peace, enthusiasm, happiness, lightness, and unconditional LOVE for Self and Others. Over time, the emotions that subtract from your happiness lose power and will eventually cease to exist in your life. Note: What you don't *feed* will eventually starve to death.
- Finally, you begin to smile . . . a lot. No, you're not cRaZy, you're just HAPPY. You're happy for no reason, and you're happy for every reason. People are drawn to you because of the light in your eyes and in your heart. You radiate LOVE, PEACE and POSITIVE energy. You begin to notice an abundance of miracles appearing in your life every day.

Be patient with yourself and the process. New thoughts, habits, and behaviors take time to digest, integrate, and develop. As long as you're committed to the ultimate goal of living "happily ever after," you will succeed. Remember, happiness is more than a feeling: happiness is a daily, conscious commitment!

Living Unconsciously—Your Obstacle to Happiness

There are only two ways to live: unconsciously or consciously. ~rln

Relax, take a deep breath, and think: What's stopping you from being happy? What's stopping you from being happy ALL THE TIME? Grab a pen and paper and list your obstacles to happiness. Answer the question from your soul, because you are the only one who has the answers. You are the only one able to create the solutions that will guarantee happiness flows to you easily and effortlessly.

First of all, there are *only* two ways to live: Unconsciously or Consciously.

Admittedly, the majority of my life was spent in an unconscious state. When you live in an unconscious state, you are dependent on a variety of events or circumstances, including other people, to "make" you happy. The stock market, your political preferences, a below-average golf game, an inconsiderate driver, the weather, your health, a rude cashier, a forgetful spouse, an anorexic bank account are a few examples of things that, according to you, determine what type of day (or life) you're having. I've labeled countless days "bad" or "good" depending on what's happened to me. Sound familiar?

If circumstances didn't match my expectations, then my day was shot to hell. Every time. Emotions like aggravation, irritation, impatience, anger, sadness, moodiness—to name a few—ruled my life. I was the queen of discontent! Sound familiar?

When I began to live consciously, my life changed dramatically. But what does "living consciously" mean, and more importantly, how do we accomplish and master living consciously twenty-four hours a day, seven days a week? Is being happy in our every waking moment even possible? I say YES, it IS possible! And I'm living proof.

Living consciously means you behave and think differently than you have in the past. Living consciously is the most important element needed for you to sustain happiness!

Example: You're driving on the freeway and someone hastily and without warning cuts into your lane, which causes you to swerve to avoid an accident. Most people would react to this situation in an unconscious manner. How would you react in this same situation? Your answer determines whether or not you respond consciously or not. Would you offer them the middle-finger salute and let the expletives fly? If that response sounds familiar or similar to how you would respond, then you are reacting unconsciously. And if you are reacting unconsciously, then that means the majority of the time, you react the same way anytime you're "disrespected" in traffic.

Does the way you react now to "disrespectful" drivers create more happiness or less happiness in your life? The answer is ... less, either certainly or more than likely.

Whenever you express anger, impatience, intolerance, or any other related emotion, you subtract from your happiness. Furthermore, you continue to subtract from your happiness as long as you choose to nurture those toxic emotions.

What are some different reactions you could choose in that same situation? I'm so glad you asked.

Let's use the same example of a driver who cuts us off in traffic, but this time let's imagine an empathetic reason why someone would drive this way. In other words, under what circumstances would you allow yourself to forgive and excuse a driver who cut you off in traffic? Are you able to come up with a plausible reason a driver might do this? If so, you are beginning to think differently. If you're stuck, let me be of some assistance.

What if the driver just received a phone call saying that his or her child, mother, husband, wife, best-friend, or grandparent was just admitted to the emergency room in a hospital fifty-five miles away? Can you imagine how you would drive with the same news? Your focus would be to get to your loved one as quickly as possible. Yes or yes?

Would you have reacted to the driver differently if you KNEW his or her circumstances? Of course you would have! So the next time someone "disrespects" you in traffic (1) Don't take their behavior personally, (2) Change your response, and (3) Notice how happier you feel.

To be clear, I'm not condoning reckless drivers. What I am saying is that if your priority is your happiness, then you have an obligation and responsibility to *you*, to consciously choose your emotions by reacting in a way that doesn't subtract from your happiness. Get it?

Practice, Practice, Practice

I find that when I'm traveling, I'm more or less forced to remain conscious. My environment has changed, and I can't rely on my *routine* behavior. Have fun and practice changing your everyday routine by changing the route you usually take to work, or shop at a different market, or change your everyday greeting. Instead of "Have a good day" or "Have a good weekend," come up with different ways to express the same sentiment. This will encourage conscious thoughts.

As with mastering any new skill, living consciously is mastered over a period of time. Remain patient with the process. Just as important is to remain patient with your *progress*. As you begin to change the way you observe and react to your circumstances, your life will change and you will be HAPPIER. As Joe Namath said, "I guarantee it!"

Happiness versus Suffering, the Choice Is Yours

Happiness is a choice we make in every moment of our day. ~rln

The vibration of suffering does not mix with the vibrations of inner peace and contentment. It's impossible to be happy and suffer and the same time. Since I have the ability to choose how I want to feel, I have chosen to eliminate suffering from my life, once and for all. Like many matters, that's easier said than done. But since inner peace and contentment (aka being happy) is my number-one priority, I decided to make eliminating internal suffering my number-two priority.

Who Defines Suffering—Man or God?

Some may point to dreaded natural disasters like hurricanes, tsunamis, earthquakes, floods, fires, et cetera, for reasons to suffer. The truth is that natural disasters constantly occur throughout the Universe—in EVERY galaxy known and unknown to man. The only difference is Earth just happens to have human beings, us, as cohabitants. Natural disasters are not a personal phenomenon. And, in my opinion, all actions of the Universe (God) are not personal. (See Universe versus Man)

When you observe the animal kingdom, nothing that happens is personal. When the lion cub is killed by a male lion who wants to mate with the female lion, it's not personal. For some penguin species, if mommy and daddy penguin have more than one chick at the same time, they instinctively care only for the strongest chick, while leaving the weakest to die. Again, it's not personal. One reason for human suffering is that we take what is undoubtedly in Universal order personally. Human beings have been conditioned and taught to take countless events and circumstances personally when, in actuality, they're not.

When you let Man define suffering, you will always find an abundance of it. However, if you let the Universe (God) define suffering, you discover there's a reason and purpose for everything—including what we call *suffering*.

When I began to know the I AM Universal Energy, my life changed. With that knowledge my suffering began to diminish. Energy cannot die or be destroyed. Our bodies will die; however, our energy lives forever. When you begin to really understand and, more importantly, embrace the basic purpose of this life, you WILL suffer less.

Do You Know Who You Are?

You are a perfect being—here at a perfect time—to experience exactly what you need to experience. There is nothing that you need to do; there is only what you are inspired to do. You are brilliantly designed. (God does not make mistakes.) You are Divine. Period.

When you begin to view the Universe (God) as impersonal Energy, this world becomes easier to understand. In fact, labels like love, suffering, sadness, joy, passion, anxiety, gratitude, loneliness, bliss, anger, depression, et cetera, are all manmade. Don't get me wrong, I'm not denying these feelings and emotions exist or saying that they're wrong. I'm merely saying Man creates all labels.

Admittedly, the goal to eliminate my own internal "suffering" is still a work-in-progress; however, I've developed a few guidelines I'd like to share with you below.

Why do I suffer? If you promise not to tell anyone, I'll share my experiences.

- I suffer when I RESIST reality.
- I suffer when I don't FLOW with this thing called Life.
- I suffer when I want something different than this moment.
- I suffer when I don't acknowledge that EVERYTHING is in perfect order.

- I suffer when I think that anything outside of me needs to change.
- I suffer when I'm in someone else's business.
- I suffer when I compare myself to others.
- I suffer when I judge.
- I suffer when I think my perspective is the only perspective.
- I suffer when I take anything seriously, including sickness and death. (I suffered when I thought death was the end of a relationship. My Father died in 2008, and I still have conversations with his Energy/Spirit.)
- I suffer when I try to control anything or anyone outside of myself.
- I suffer when I allow my ego to make choices—other than what outfit, hairstyle, or lipstick to wear.
- I suffer when I think my plan is better than the Universe's plan.
- I suffer when I have an attachment to an outcome.
- I suffer when I have expectations.
- I suffer when I avoid looking for the Truth. (Usually, that's coupled with looking in the mirror.)

I could go on and on, but, hopefully, you get my point. Internal suffering is a manmade condition; therefore, internal suffering can be un-made. The great news is we all have a choice.

I choose to be happy! You?

CHAPTER 2

Universe versus Man

There's a significant difference between what the Universe creates and what Man creates. When you align yourself with what the Universe creates, you immediately feel peace of mind. When you align yourself with what Man creates, you're screwed. What's the difference between Universal creations and manmade creations? I say you instinctually know the answer if you close your eyes, drop your shoulders, relax, and breathe through the moment.

Years ago, I created a spiritual game. I call it Universe versus Man (UvM). It's a game I use to help me remain on the Happiness Train whenever I'm challenged by this thing we call life. To play, all you have to do is ask yourself one simple question: Who created it—Man or the Universe?

Pop Quiz: Answer the questions below with Yes or No.

- Do you think the Universe cares about how you look?

- Do you think the Universe cares about how much money you make?
- Do you think the Universe cares about how much you weigh, or how old you are, or your education level?
- Do you think the Universe cares about your title?
- This is a more challenging question: do you think the Universe judges? Let's take a closer look at whether or not this is true.

The Pope and the Serial Killer

The pope and a serial killer enter a greenhouse filled with beautiful garden flowers. The floral scents are intoxicating. There are tulips, daisies, carnations, orchids, and daffodils in bloom. The only thing missing in our imaginary greenhouse are roses. Each man plants a single bush of red roses side by side at the same time. Both men fertilize and water their roses every week at the same time. Can you tell me which rose bush is going to bloom?

The Universe does not make a judgment as to whose roses are going to bloom. The sun shines on both rose bushes. Both bushes bloom and produce beautiful award-winning red roses. What's my point? *We* were not born with the *skill* to judge. Judgment is a manmade behavior (UvM). Let's go back to the questions I asked above.

- Do you think the Universe cares about how you look?

RealitySpirituality: The Truth About Happiness

- Do you think the Universe cares about how much money you make?
- Do you think the Universe cares about how much you weigh, or how old you are, or your education level?
- Do you think the Universe cares about your title?

If you've studied "Spirituality 101," you know the answer to all of the above questions is an emphatic NO! The Universe doesn't compute nor recognize the above manmade concepts and expectations. But Man does. That's why I choose to align with concepts of the Universe, and the Universe alone.

I was brainwashed to think that if I didn't live up to manmade expectations, I wasn't successful. Successful by whose standards; and, more importantly, who defines success? Example: If I wasn't married, there was something wrong. If I was married and didn't have any children, there was something wrong. When you align with team M.A.N., there'll never be a shortage of judgments to choose from. All judgments are manmade; and when you judge, you choose to subtract from your happiness. Why would I want to indulge in a behavior that subtracts from my happiness? That's CrAzY!

When I developed the new habit of recognizing the differences between Man-consciousness and Universal-consciousness, it became really easy for me to choose the team I want to play for.

The Universe LOVES, regardless of what you do; and the Universe LOVES, regardless of what you don't do. During the last couple of years, I've applied this philosophy to everyone in my life, from family and friends to co-workers. I'm thrilled to share this: ALL of my relationships have improved. I love, regardless of what they do or say; and I love, regardless of what they don't do or say.

Because...

- When you know you are eternal, you will develop unwavering patience.
- When you know everything is in order, you will develop trust.
- When you know everything that happens "to" you has an ultimate purpose for your betterment, you will develop wisdom.
- When you know there is nothing you have to do, that there is only what you are inspired to do, you will develop peace.
- When you know who you really are, you will always be happy.

Go Team Universe! Cost of Admission: Choose to be Happy!

Realms of the Universe

This Universe is vast and complex. Even though I am a physical extension of the Universe, I am limited in my understanding because I am also human. I do not know how many realms or dimensions exist in the Universe, but I would imagine there is an infinite amount. On January 12, 2014, the

Universe spoke to me and shared information about two of the realms: the realm of *Knowing* and the realm of *Thinking*. With that said, I'm going to describe, to the best of my ability, what I heard while I was sitting alone quietly.

The Realm of Knowing

In the realm of Knowing, you know everything. You know the reason for all existence. You know the reason why everything exists. In the realm of Knowing, forms/entities are able to insert themselves into other forms/entities and know exactly what that form/entity is experiencing, feeling, and thinking.

It is impossible for me to know exactly what another person is experiencing unless I am that person. It is impossible for me to feel what another person is feeling unless I am that person. It is impossible for me to think what that person is thinking unless I am that person. There is no thinking in the realm of Knowing.

If you or I lived in the realm of Knowing, we would be able to insert ourselves into any form of energy and become that form. We do not live in the realm of Knowing, and because we do not live in that realm, it is impossible for us to know anything except ourselves and the Laws of the Universe.

The Realm of Thinking

There are thousands, perhaps millions, of events happening that we are not aware of at any given time. There are sounds that we cannot hear. There are substances that we cannot see. There is movement, creation, and expansion that we do not knowingly experience. The room that we are sitting in now is filled with microscopic *beings* invisible to the human eyes. Dark matter and dark energy have not been explained. Scientists know of the existence of dark energy and dark matter, but for now that's all we know. The energy in the room that you are currently in has an affect on you. But you do not know what affect that is. You cannot know, because you are living in the realm of Thinking. There is only so much you can see and there is only so much you can hear and only so much you can experience. If we lived in the realm of Knowing, we would know all that exists. But we live in the realm of Thinking. The realm of Thinking is limited.

The realm of Thinking has a specific purpose. The realm of Thinking is to be experienced and enjoyed. The realm of Thinking exists for expansion. Expansion of thinking. Expansion of feeling. The realm of Thinking requests that you release all that you think you know. Release your name. Release your age. Release your gender. Release the pressure of thinking you know.

In the realm of Thinking, the ego insists on knowing. The ego will try to convince you that you know. (The ego is only as powerful as you allow it to be.)

What Is Real and What Is an Illusion?

The reality is... "There is no spoon." – The Matrix (1999 movie)

Have you ever had a nightmare that was so upsetting you believed it was real? Especially when you were in the middle of it? That's happened to me more times than I can or want to remember. It's never a good feeling to have an upsetting dream also known as a nightmare. When I awaken and realize that it was just a dream, the relief I feel can be measured on the Richter scale. I don't know how traumatic emotions and or feelings work their way into my dreams, but I can vouch for the fact that I feel them. Thank goodness that when I wake up, I'm instantly able to let go of all the traumatic emotions that plagued me in the dream. And I mean instantly. There isn't one reason why I would want to bring feelings like worry, anxiety, trauma, stress, or fear into my day. Which brings me to the question: what is real and what is an illusion?

How do we define what is real? How do we determine what to give our focus to? These are important questions that can only be answered by you, the individual. We all are as different as our fingerprints, and I do not pretend to know the answers for you. I do, however, know what I define and determine to be real, and I also know what I define and determine to be an illusion.

I spent thirty-plus years of my life focusing on, in my opinion, what is not real. I spent thirty-plus years expressing emotions in my day-to-day life that are found in most nightmares, which means the nightmarish emotions I felt were based on illusions rather than on reality. As my father would say, "Now you tell me." What about you? Do you spend precious time in your day focusing on illusions rather than reality?

Let me share with you what I define as Illusion.

- **Time is an illusion.** Time is a manmade concept. There is no such thing as a *finite* amount of time in the universe. Therefore, it is impossible to waste time. How can you waste what you have an infinite supply of? *I used to always feel like I was wasting time. Not anymore.*
- **Death is an illusion.** Everything is energy. Energy can change forms, but Energy cannot be created or destroyed. You and I are Energy in a physical body. Our physical body will eventually deteriorate, but the essence or *reality* of who and what we are (Energy) will never die. Therefore, why would I choose to be sad when someone dies? *I used to believe the death of a person was the end of their life. Not anymore.*
- **Being offended is an illusion.** You cannot be offended unless you believe the offense. If you believe the offense, then it's your responsibility to change your belief, unless you "enjoy" being offended. You will never be able to control what someone else says—ever. Which type of person is more powerful? Someone who can be offended or someone it is impossible to offend? *I used to be offended by the way the wind blew. I chose to evolve into an entity that could not be affected by mere words.*
- **All labels are illusions.** We put labels on life all the time: Right, wrong, good, bad, successful, lazy, lucky, unlucky.

Labels are illusions based on a subjective opinion. When you label you actually limit your experience. Think about it. What if you awakened as a clean slate every day from now on? (This is not like the movie *Groundhog Day*, because in the movie, Bill Murray retained his ability to label.)

If you didn't have the ability to label, you would experience all that happens as new moments. Your perception of Self would be without limits. Expectations would be eliminated. (All expectations subtract from happiness.) *During the last year, I have practiced eliminating all labels. It's become one of my favorite daily practices that continue to add to my happiness.*

There are many more illusions to recognize in your own life. Are you able to name a few? It's extremely important to be consciously aware of what's real and what is an illusion, because when you are aware, you will be able to choose your focus.

- I AM a physical extension of the Universe
- I AM as unique as my fingerprints
- I do not have to "do" anything to be happy
- The present moment is my only reality
- My purpose is to grow, evolve and be happy

CHAPTER 3

Everything Is Energy

Everything is made of energy. The same energy that creates worlds creates us. Energy will and has always existed in one form or another. Energy cannot be created and it cannot be destroyed. It's in constant flow, changing form all the time. Everything we do, think, and say involves some type of energy. Our personal spirit, our thoughts, our bodies, and our emotions are all forms of energy. Everything that happens in the Universe, from a volcano erupting to a seed sprouting, to people walking and talking, is energy. Your personal energy or vibration has a direct influence on your life. This knowledge is essential to understanding why you feel and react the way you do.

This information is not a new discovery. Throughout history, there are different cultures that have recognized and practiced ways to work with self-energy. For example, the Chinese practice Tai Chi. People in India practice kundalini awakening. In Japan, they practice Reiki. All three practices focus on personal energy.

The Importance of Understanding the Laws of the Universe

The Laws of the Universe have been scientifically and mathematically proven to exist. They are automatically operating, regardless of whether you believe they exist or not. No one is exempt from the Laws affecting their life. When I realized, without one doubt, that Universal Laws play a dominate role in my daily life, I was forced to make a lot of changes. I was forced to change my destructive thoughts. I was forced to change my damaging behaviors. I was even forced to change the way I spoke to myself and to others. There were words I was compelled to delete from my vocabulary. Yes, when I discovered the truth about the Laws of the Universe, time began to run out on my recycled thoughts and behaviors. Living unconsciously was no longer an option for me.

Like most changes that "stick," my transformation did not happen overnight. In fact, it's an ongoing process—an endless journey. Just like the evolution of the Universe, I am constantly evolving into someone I wasn't yesterday.

The Laws of the Universe affect us all, on a daily basis. Acknowledging and, more importantly, utilizing the laws will create major change in your own life.

The Laws of the Universe

The Seven Universal Laws offered here were taken, in part, from Tania Kotsos' article on her Mind Your Reality Website, which she attributes to having been based on information from two books: *The Science of Being* and *The Kybalion*. Comments in italics are solely mine.

There are seven Universal Laws or Principles by which everything in the Universe is governed. The Universe exists in perfect harmony by virtue of these Laws. Ancient mystical, esoteric, and secret teachings dating back over 5,000 years from Ancient Egypt to Ancient Greece and to the Vedic tradition of Ancient India, all have as their common thread, these seven Spiritual Laws of the Universe. Once you understand, apply, and align yourself with these Universal Laws, you will experience transformation in every area of your life, beyond that which you have ever dared to imagine.

Immutable and Mutable Laws

Of the seven Universal Laws, the first three are immutable, eternal Laws, meaning they are Absolute and can never be changed or transcended. They have always existed and will always exist. The other four laws are transitory, mutable Laws, meaning that they can be transcended or at least "better used" to create your ideal reality. Learning how to transcend the mutable Laws is fundamental to changing the circumstances of your life so that you can consciously create an intended reality and achieve true mastery. Your aim is to master each of the seven Universal Laws and then learn to transcend the mutable ones.

1. The Law of Mentalism (Immutable)

The first of the seven Universal Laws tells us that "The All is Mind—The Universe is Mental." That everything we see and experience in our physical world has its origin in the invisible mental realm. It tells us that there is a single Universal Consciousness—the Universal Mind—from which all things manifest. All energy and matter, at all levels, is created by and is subordinate to the Omnipresent Universal Mind. Your mind is part of the Universal Mind—the same in kind, with the only difference being one of degree. Your reality is a manifestation of your mind.

2. The Law of Correspondence (Immutable)

The second of the seven Universal Laws tells us "As above, so below; as below, so above." This means that there is "harmony, agreement, and correspondence" between the physical, mental, and spiritual realms. There is no separation, since everything in the Universe, including you, originates from the One Source. The same pattern is expressed on all planes of existence, from the smallest electron to the largest star, and vice versa. All is One. The ancient Greek Temple of Apollo at Delphi was referring to this great Law of Correspondence in the inscription, "Know thyself and thou shalt know all the mysteries of the gods and the Universe."

3. The Law of Vibration (Immutable)

The third of the seven Universal Laws tells us that "Nothing rests; everything moves; everything vibrates." The third and last of the immutable Universal Laws tells us that "the whole universe is but a vibration." Science has confirmed that everything in the Universe, including you, is pure energy vibrating at different frequencies.

The axiom that "like energy attracts like energy," upon which the Law of Attraction is based, has its foundation in this Law. Everything that we experience with our five physical senses is conveyed through vibrations. The same applies to the mental realm: Your thoughts are vibrations. All of your emotions are vibrations, where "unconditional love" (in the sense of love for another) is the highest and most subtle of the emotional vibrations. "Hate" is the densest and most base vibration. You can learn to control your mental vibrations at will. This is true thought-power.

Your Personal Vibration

The Universe is always responding to your personal vibration. Your personal vibration determines who and what you attract. I like to make the analogy of listening to the radio. When you listen to the radio, you choose a specific station—music, talk, sports, news, traffic, et cetera. Your choice depends on what you want to hear. Let's say the station on the radio is the same as, that is, it parallels our personal vibration. What's your favorite station? What do you choose to listen to throughout your day? Are you tuning into 101.3 FM Complaining? 98.7 AM Blaming? 570 AM Anger with a dose of Irritation? 103.2 FM Negativity and Destructive Drama? Or do you choose to "set" your personal vibration to Unconditional Love for Self and Others? Are you choosing to vibrate the energy of allowing, acceptance, flowing, trust, and surrender—without resistance?

How do you measure your personal vibration during any given moment throughout your day? There's an easy way to determine your personal vibration. You measure your vibration based on how you FEEL. Our feelings and our emotions can be scientifically measured and are direct indicators of our personal vibration. I like to think of my personal vibration as a thermostat—a personal thermostat that I set to whichever station I choose.

If your personal vibration is "low," then you are more likely to exhibit anger, become moody, practice worry, be stressed or anxious while feeling sad, depressed, neglected, discouraged, fearful, alone, et cetera. By emitting a lower vibration or frequency, you never really experience a peaceful and happy life... It is impossible. As with developing any skill, it is not easy to raise your vibration overnight. Raising your vibration requires an unwavering daily commitment from you; but trust me: it is worth it.

When your personal vibration is "high," you are more likely to feel optimistic, grateful, competent, confidant, purposeful, valued, appreciated, LOVED, and connected. When you are able to maintain a high personal vibration, you develop the ability to be happy regardless of external circumstances. In addition, your thoughts and behaviors have more effectiveness when you act from a positive state as opposed to a negative one. An added bonus is that your positive energy, along with your higher vibration, acts as a ripple effect throughout the world. Because you have raised your vibration, you have actually changed the world without even leaving home.

4. The Law of Polarity (Mutable)

The fourth of the seven Universal Laws tells us that "Everything is dual, everything has poles; everything has its pair of opposites; opposites are identical in nature, but different in degree." It is also the first of the mutable, or can be transcended, Universal Laws. It means that there are two sides to everything. Things that appear as opposites are in fact only two extremes of the same thing. For instance, hot and cold may appear to be opposites at first glance, but in truth they are simply varying degrees of the same thing: temperature. The same applies to love and hate, peace and war, positive and negative, good and evil, yes and no, light and dark, energy and matter. You can transform your thoughts from hate to love or from fear to courage by consciously raising your vibration. This is what in the ancient Hermetic teachings is called the Art of Polarization.

Rising above the Law of Polarity: This Principle of Duality may appear to be very real in your life, but it operates only in the physical and mental realms, not in the spiritual realm where All is One. As it says in the *Bhagavad-Gita*, "God is Above the Opposites." By always placing the all-powerful, all-knowing Great Spirit of which you are a part of behind your every thought, statement, and action, and by always focusing on the "good," even when things appear to be going "bad," in time you will rise above the Law of Polarity.

5. The Law of Rhythm (Mutable)

The fifth of the seven Universal Laws tells us that "Everything flows, out and in; everything has its tides; all things rise and fall; the pendulum-swing manifests in everything; the measure of the swing to the right is the measure of the swing to the left; rhythm compensates." It is the second of the mutable, or can be transcended, Universal Laws, and means that the pendulum swings for everything. This principle can be seen in operation in the waves of the ocean, in the rise and fall of the greatest empires, in business cycles, in the swaying of your thoughts from being positive to negative, and in your personal successes and failures. In accordance with this Law, when anything reaches a point of culmination, then the backward swing begins almost unnoticeably, until such time that any forward movement has been totally reversed. Then the forward movement begins again and the process is repeated.

Rising above the Law of Rhythm: To transcend the swing of the pendulum, you must become aware of the subtle start of the backward movement in any of your endeavors, whether it be to improve your health, your finances, your relationships, or any goal you may set in motion. When you feel the Law start to draw you back, do not become fearful or discouraged. Instead, know that you are one with the Omnipotent Universal Mind for which nothing is impossible; keep your thoughts focused on your outcome; and fight to remain positive, no matter how far back this transitory Law pulls you. Even if your efforts meet with failure, find comfort that by virtue of this very same Law, the upward motion must start again. In time, your perseverance will be rewarded as the backward movements become less negative relative to your previous backward swings and you raise yourself higher.

6. The Law of Cause and Effect (Mutable)

The sixth of the seven Universal Laws tells us that "Every cause has its effect; every effect has its cause." In accordance with this Law, every effect you see in your outside or physical world has a very specific cause, which has its origin in your inner or mental world. This is the essence of thought power. Every one of your thoughts, words, or actions sets a specific effect in motion which will come to materialize over time. To become the master of your destiny, you must master your mind, because everything in your reality is a mental creation. Know that there is nothing like chance or luck. They are simply terms used by humanity in ignorance of this Law.

Your Intentions are Instantly Created: The Law of Cause and Effect applies on all three planes of existence: the spiritual, the mental, and the physical. The difference is that on the spiritual plane, cause and effect are instantaneous such that they appear inseparable; whereas, on the other planes, our concept of time and space creates a time lag between the cause and the eventual effect. Know that when you focus on your chosen goals with intention, and using creative visualization, that which you want to create in the physical world is automatically manifested in the spiritual world; and with perseverance, practice, and continued concentrated thought, it will also come to materialize in the physical world.

7. The Law of Gender (Mutable)

The last of the seven Universal Laws tells us that "Gender is in everything; everything has its masculine and feminine principles." This Universal Law is evident throughout creation in the so-called opposite sexes found not only in human beings but also in plants, minerals, electrons, and magnetic poles, to name but a few. Everything and everyone contains both masculine and feminine elements. Among the outward expressions of feminine qualities are love, patience, intuition, and gentleness; and of masculine qualities are energy, self-reliance, logic, and intellect. Know that within every woman reside all the latent qualities of a man; and within every man, those of a woman. When you know this, you will know what it means to be complete.

The Law of Attraction Is Part of the Equation

You will notice that the Law of Attraction is not specifically mentioned as one of the seven Universal Laws. This is not to diminish its importance, but rather to highlight it, because the Law of Attraction is the basic Law of the Universe that runs through all the seven Universal Laws discussed here. It holds everything together. It is through knowledge of the Law of Attraction that one can rise above the mutable Laws of Polarity and Rhythm and gain a better understanding of each of the seven Universal Laws.

The Mental Laws

Here is a summary of The Mental Laws from the book *The Awakening Human Being – A Guide to the Power of Mind* by Barbara Berger with Tim Ray. The Mental Laws are summarized here with the authors' permission. Comments in italics are mine.

The Importance of Understanding Mental Laws

This information is important because without this understanding, we can easily become victims of our minds instead of the masters of our lives.

Once you understand the mental laws and the way the mind works, you understand why you experience life the way you do. And when this happens, you will also see what you can realistically change in your life and what you cannot change. Plus, you will also better understand the difference between reality (what is actually happening right now) and your thinking and this discovery will lead you to an ever-deepening understanding of who/what you really are.

What is a Law?

A law is an unchanging principle that describes the way phenomena operate. There are laws which describe the way physical phenomena operate and there are laws which describe the way mental phenomena operate. Whether a law is describing physical or mental phenomena, a law is always a description of an impersonal sequence of events which is not dependent on the person or people involved in that sequence of events. In addition, laws can be observed and confirmed by anyone.

The law of gravity is a good example of a physical law. As you know, the law of gravity is impersonal and it is always operating. Because of this law, if you jump off a building, you will immediately fall to the ground. There are no exceptions to this law. It doesn't matter who you are or how much money you have in the bank or how famous you are, because the law is impersonal and operates regardless of the situation, time of year, or the people involved. There are no exceptions to the law. Another important thing about a law is that it is in operation whether you are aware of it or not. In other words, if you jump off a building, you are going to fall and hit the ground whether you know about the law of gravity or not. The law doesn't care if you know about the law or not. The law just operates; it is a blind force of nature.

The same goes for mental laws. They are impersonal and simply describe the way our minds work. Anyone can observe and confirm this information. So when reading about the mental laws, it is a good idea to remember that laws are invisible principles that describe how phenomena behave and that laws operate automatically. (You can't make them happen or not happen.) Laws are impersonal. (It doesn't matter who you are.) Laws operate equally for all. And finally—laws are scientific. (They can be observed and confirmed by anyone.)

1. The Law Of Thoughts Arising

Thoughts arise and disappear. This is the first law because it describes an impersonal universal phenomenon which is true for everyone. No one knows why or where thoughts come from or what a thought is, but everyone has thoughts. Thoughts come and go on their own. It happens to everyone and that is why this is a law. It's an impersonal phenomenon. And it is happening all the time—to everyone—in every waking hour of our lives.

2. The Law Of Witnessing

There is a difference between you and your thoughts. There is a difference between you, the one who is having thoughts, and the thoughts themselves. The discovery—that there is a difference between you and your thoughts—is so important because it is the key to freedom, unlimited insights, greater understanding, and in the end—total liberation from whatever is bothering you. When you realize that there is a difference between you and your thoughts—you start to witness and examine your thoughts instead of being run by them.

How do I co-exist with my thoughts? I visualize that my thoughts are on stage and I am sitting in the audience enjoying a not-so-real reality show. Sometimes the show is filled with drama. Sometimes the show is hilarious. Sometimes the show is sad. Sometimes the show is all bad news. Whatever the show (aka my thoughts) are, I know that it's just a show—an illusion. Illusions are not real. More importantly, regardless of what type of show I'm watching, I still choose how I want to feel. My thoughts do not dictate my feelings or my behavior. My feelings and my behavior are always my choice.

3. The Law Of Naming

Thoughts name the world. Naming is a global occurrence. No one escapes it. When we are born, we have no language. And then our parents teach us how to name and label everything. That's how we all begin. We name and label the world and then we start telling stories about it. And then our stories become more complex and we begin to make judgments, decisions, and conclusions about our stories.

And then we label our stories "good," "bad," "right," and "wrong," and we believe the labels we have attached to each story.

Where did feelings of unhappiness originate? In my opinion, the origin of unhappiness began as soon as man placed a value on the labels we use. As soon as a value of labels surfaced, feelings of dissatisfaction and unhappiness were born.

4. The Law Of Cause And Effect

Thought is cause, experience is effect. Our thinking—the thoughts that we entertain—determine our experience of life. In brief, this means that our experiences are the result of our thoughts about life or reality—and not the result of experiencing reality itself directly. This law means: Whatever you think, you get to experience. When you think something is great, you get to experience that. When you think something is terrible, you get to experience that. The discovery is, everything we experience is the effect of our thinking.

All of our thoughts and actions have consequences. That's why the Law of Cause and Effect keeps me in check.

5. The Law Of Emotion

You cannot have an emotion without having a thought first. The order in which emotions occur is always—thoughts first—then the emotional reaction—and then the physical reaction. You cannot be angry without having an angry thought first. You cannot be sad without having a sad thought first. It's just not possible. You cannot feel loving and kind about anything or anyone without having loving and kind thoughts first. Understanding that thought precedes emotion will help us understand that we alone are responsible for our own experiences. We are not victims of outside forces which are beyond our control, but rather that we are experiencing our own unconscious thoughts and programming.

There was a time in my life when my emotions dictated how I felt and, more importantly, how I behaved. I never knew I was able to choose my emotions, until I understood the mechanics of emotions.

6. The Law Of Focus

Whatever you focus your attention on grows. This is a very empowering discovery. It means we energize whatever we focus our attention on. Our attention "brings to life" out of the vast field of infinite energy or pure potentiality whatever we focus on. [This has now been confirmed by Quantum mechanics which has proven that observation by a conscious observer is responsible for the collapse of the wave function (Heisenberg principle) into actual particles in the field of potentiality.] Ask yourself—what is the general tone of your thinking? Is it a praiseful song of gratitude from morning to evening for the blessings of life—or is it one long complaint? If you look carefully (and are honest) you will see that your experience is a perfect reflection of your focus. If you focus on lack, you will experience lack. If you focus on the abundance of your life, you will experience abundance. If you focus on love, you will experience love.

If you are not feeling good as a result of how you're focusing your attention, change how you focus your attention.

7. The Law Of Free Will

You can choose. You are the only thinker in your mind. It is the key to freedom—the high road. Because when you understand this, you also understand that you can become the conscious choice-maker in your life and choose. No one else can make a choice for you. The ability to choose the focus of our attention is one of our greatest gifts. It is the gift of free will. Free will is our true nature, our essence.

You are powerful. Free yourself.

8. The Law Of Underlying Beliefs

Your underlying beliefs determine your experience. Reality is what it is. Life is what it is. But our experience of this thing called life is determined by our thoughts and underlying beliefs about life—whether or not we are conscious of this mechanism. Our basic beliefs about life determine our experience of reality. These basic, underlying beliefs are something we learn from early childhood from parents, society, teachers, media, religion and culture. From the moment we are born, we are programmed by the society we are born into—we learn the belief systems of our family and culture. Unfortunately, these beliefs can wreak havoc on our lives—until we begin to be aware of them and learn to question their validity.

What you believed yesterday and what you believe today can change tomorrow.

9. The Law Of Substitution

Change your thinking, change your life. The law of substitution tells us you can only change your thinking by replacing old thoughts and thought patterns with new ones.

It's almost impossible to force yourself to stop thinking a certain thought, but you can substitute that thought with a new one. Practice substituting your negative thoughts with thoughts that serve you.

10. The Law Of Mental Equivalents

Like attracts like. This law explains that everything we experience in the world is a reflection of the mental equivalents we hold in thought. In other words, all our experiences in the "outer" world are merely equivalent reflections of our "inner" state of mind, or consciousness. Have you ever noticed that a person's experiences match their state of mind? Your present experience always reflects your present state of mind.

For a person who is annoyed quickly, irritation appears around every corner. Angry people experience countless moments to feed their anger. People who consistently complain are never out of topics to complain about. Negative, critical, and resentful people are magnets for the same type of circumstances. On the other hand, people who are open, honest, generous, loving, and kind will attract the same energy to them. Become what you want to attract.

11. The Mental Law Of Truth

No thoughts are true. Because your thoughts are not reality. They are just thoughts. The truth is reality is not what we think. Thoughts and reality are two separate things. All human suffering comes from identifying, attaching, and believing thoughts that are not true. If we did not believe what we think, it would be impossible to suffer.

Accept that your thoughts are not true and change your life.

CHAPTER 4

The Purpose of Life

The purpose of Life is to experience joy and evolve. ~rln

In my not-so-humble opinion, the purpose of life is to (1) learn and accept ourselves, and then (2) evolve from what we've learned. Yes, we are here to become aware of our true status: We are all physical extensions of the Universe. We are spiritual beings living in a human body. Anytime we view ourselves as less than that, we suffer. I've discovered that there's no end to this remarkable journey; and I, for one, am grateful for the ability to recognize the Truth.

The Meaning of Life

The meaning of life is quite different than the purpose of life; however, they both are Universally linked together. The meaning of life is to share *you* with as many people as possible. What does that mean? Sharing *you* means sharing who you were born to be. Sharing that two-year-old with the world. I use the analogy of a two-year-old because at the age of two, I hadn't learned how to be critical, judgmental, or dissatisfied with myself—yet. At two, I was curious, eager to explore, playful, creative, happy, content, and admittedly easy to please. I was easy to get along with, unless I needed food, sleep, or a change of diapers.

At two years of age, my significance, worthiness, and value was never questioned by me or anyone else. Of course, I don't remember exactly when I began thinking of myself in an uncomplimentary light, but I do know that it happened. I know it happened because of how unhappy I was.

What's So Important?

Years ago I volunteered as an activity director in an assisted-living home. I was given an opportunity to spend two hours each week planning activities like chair aerobics, sing-a-longs, simple games, et cetera. As you can imagine, the majority of residents were in their seventies, eighties, and nineties.

I remember thinking that all of these people had been fortunate enough to make it to this stage in their lives, and I became curious to find out more about each person. Specifically, what did a seventy-, eighty-, or ninety-year-old think was important? I was in my thirties at the time, and I was sure that what I thought was important was not important to them. So, I did what I always do when I want information: I asked. The following week I decided to schedule an hour to listen to what my new friends wanted in their lives. I wanted to learn what was really important to them. I arranged some chairs in a circle so that everyone was able to have eye contact with one another. I asked them, one by one, "If you could have anything in the world, what would it be?" I walked around the circle repeating this question to each of the twenty-five seated people.

The majority of the people wanted better health. A few people wanted a companion. Some expressed a desire to travel. One woman's response was unforgettable. She said, "I want my own car. I want to be able to drive again." Of course, I needed to ask her the million-dollar follow-up question, "Why?" She replied, "I don't see my daughter anymore, because she moved to another city forty-five minutes away. She doesn't visit me as often as she used to; and if I had my own car, I would be able to drive to see her."

Her answer made a profound impact on my life. From that day forward, I consciously made changes as to what I thought was really important in *my* life. Her answer changed the frequency of my interactions with my parents. In fact, when my parents retired and moved 275 miles away, I visited them more than when they'd lived in the same town as me.

CHAPTER 5

Happiness: Mission Possible—Only if You're Willing to Lose Control

When you attempt to control anything or anyone outside of Self, you subtract from your happiness. ~ rln

There are countless reasons why people are not as happy as they can be. In this section I'd like to share what I've discovered to be a couple of foundational reasons for unhappiness.

First, let me be clear: The happiness I'm talking about has nothing to do with an event you've experienced or a situation you've found yourself in or even a relationship with another person. No, the happiness I'm referring to is internal happiness. It's a feeling of peace *in* mind, regardless of what you're outwardly experiencing. Peace coupled with unwavering contentment.

Internal happiness is different from external happiness. Internal happiness is ETERNAL. External happiness comes and goes with time, people, events, and circumstances. And, thank God for that! Why? Because when I relied on external circumstances to determine my happiness, my life experience resembled a roller coaster ride . . . up, down; up, down; up, down. And to make it worse, the frickin' ride never ended! I'd still be onboard today if I hadn't become sick and tired of feeling sick and tired. It wasn't until I couldn't bear that feeling any longer that I went in search of a new way to live. However, as it is with most thrill-rides, this new *ride* came with a WARNING:

"When you choose to give up *emotional roller coasters*, you MUST give up habitual ways of thinking and behaving. If not, you might as well stay on the ride."

Okay, I'm willing to try anything to feel better, I thought to myself. "What will I have to give up first?" I meekly asked.

"You MUST give up the need to control anyone and anything."

"Why?"

"Trying to Control Anyone or Anything Leads to Unhappiness."

"Yikes! Who knew?"

"My name is Rebecca L. Norrington, and I'm a recovering Controloholic!"

Admittedly, I've spent decades determined to control everything and everybody that crossed my path. Controlling external events is like trying to control a tsunami: Mission Impossible! Further, why did I have the need to control anything and everyone outside of me? The answer was simple: I didn't know I had other options. I didn't know I could choose another type of behavior. I was only mirroring what I'd witnessed as a child.

I actually believed that if I loved someone, it was my responsibility to tell him or her what to do. My mother and father always told me what to do and what to think. I was ignorantly keeping that behavior alive! More importantly, I had no clue that attempting to control anyone or anything other than myself would subtract from my happiness. I was constantly shooting myself in the foot, so to speak. Besides, *I* knew what was right. I especially *knew* what was right for everybody else. Yes, I spent a lot of time thinking and voicing my strong opinions about what others should do. "Listen to me; I know what's best for you! Listen to *meee!*"

It's funny, though . . . because with all of the controlling skills I'd mastered, I was still miserable. As an example, when my "orders" weren't followed and my suggestions were ignored, my "subjects" had major problems. Yes, they all had consequences to pay. The consequences ranged from high-pitched tongue-lashings to total exile. *That'll show them . . . Try living without me!*

Trying to Control Anything or Anyone Leads to Unhappiness

For me, giving up control didn't happen overnight. I went out kicking and screaming. In fact, after years of detoxifying myself of control issues, I'm still in *rehab* on an out-patient basis. Admittedly, there are times when I feel the need for a cheap thrill-ride; however, it's not the same experience anymore. I actually feel uncomfortable wearing my former controller hat. After years of practice and patience, the old roller coaster has lost its draw and sparkle. What I can say is this: I've never been happier.

Mastering Self—My Greatest Accomplishment

What if I told you that you have the power to create heaven on Earth when you MASTER SELF? Would you believe it? If not, let me explain.

YOU are the most powerful person in the Universe! More importantly, you don't have to search for your power. Your power lives WITHIN. Your power is your birthright, and you have the ability to access it in any moment. Accessing your power and making choices that serve you is my definition of "self-mastery." Mastering SELF includes mastering emotions, behaviors, and actions.

In any given moment in any given day, you are making choices. To clarify, I'm not referring to which restaurant you choose or which outfit makes you look slimmer. No, I'm talking about your day-to-day choices made while interacting with the world.

As an example, let me share a personal story.

Shhhhh ... Don't tell anyone ... I love to drive, and I love to drive really fast! I could have been a race car driver; however, my parents wanted me to finish school, so consequently, I was sidetracked. Anyway, back to the story. I pass cars all the time that aren't moving as fast as I need them to travel. I admit there have been several instances, while passing a slower motorist, when I've received the famous "one-finger salute." I never understood why passing a stranger on the road invoked such a passionate response; however, I've accepted this phenomenon for what it is—a reaction from a stranger, which I refuse to take personally.

Recently, I was routinely driving to the bus station where I park my car before riding the remaining distance on public transportation into downtown Los Angeles. What happened next was not routine.

I was stopped at a traffic signal. There were three lanes of southbound traffic, and I was positioned in the far right lane. As soon as the light turned green, I shot out like the first horse out of the gate at a race track. I floored the pedal to the metal as I began to pass the motorist on my left. Well, the driver on my left side rejected my Mario Andretti maneuver and refused to let me pass. In fact, without warning, he violently turned his steering wheel toward my automobile! It was a dangerous and blatant attempt to force me off the road. Unlike my memory, my reflexes still remain quick and sharp. I immediately jammed on the brakes and turned my steering wheel to the right, to avoid hitting him and the curb ahead.

I'm sure you can imagine several ways a person could choose to react at such a moment; however, I did not choose any of the typical ones. I chose to do something that was out of the norm for me: a response that required a connection with the Universe. Can you guess which response I'm describing?

Admittedly, my adrenaline was pumping while I swerved off the road to avoid a collision. After coming to a stop, I took a few deep breaths and gathered my thoughts. I recovered quickly and began my intended journey to the bus station.

Well, guess who I ran into (pun intended) on the way to my final destination? Yes, as fate would have it, Mr. Road Rage was stopped at the next traffic signal.

I drove directly behind Mr. R. Rage and snapped a picture of his license plate with my iPhone, just in case. The light turned green. I changed lanes to position myself directly on his left side. We traveled side by side for approximately a half mile, before another traffic signal stopped us.

As Mr. R. Rage stopped for the light, he drove his car forward, past the crosswalk, far enough to practically reach the intersection. I did the same. He knew I was next to him, and he was avoiding any contact. I rolled down my passenger window while he continued to stare straight ahead. I then tapped on the horn (*toot-toot*) to get his attention. He ignored me. I tapped again, *toot-toot*. He finally looked my way; and when our eyes met, I clasped my hands together in a submissive praying position. My demeanor was calm. I motioned for him to roll his window down, and after a few seconds he did so, reluctantly. I began with, "Sir, I was almost in an accident because of the way you changed lanes." I continued in my sweetest voice, "Please be careful!" My hands were still in the prayer position. At that moment we were looking directly into each other's eyes. The attempted murderer (insert happy face here) was momentarily confused and lost for words. He wasn't expecting this chosen response. I gave him a reassuring smile; and he said—*wait for it—wait for it,* "I'm sorry. I didn't see you." I quickly offered, "Okay, no problem. Thank you, and drive safely." I flashed the Universal peace sign and drove off. At that moment, I needed to check my rearview mirror to make sure I was the one speaking, because years ago I would have used several expletives, along with threats to have him arrested for attempted murder!

Now, his statement, "I didn't see you," was untrue and his actions had been deliberate. However, I chose to ignore the evidence in order to create what is more important to me—a sense of internal peace. This is when the practice of self-mastery comes into play: acknowledging I am the sole individual responsible for my personal state.

Self-mastery is about creating and maintaining a tone, a personal environment, if you will, for self. You are the only one who has control over you. You don't have control over outside forces or what happens to you because of outside forces.

Your power lies in your CHOICES. You have the power to change your attitude and change your reaction into a response about anything that has happened, is happening, or will happen to you!

Please take note that I said change your attitude and change your reaction to what happens in your life—not the circumstances. This truth is a very important concept to accept. Your ability to give up trying to control anything outside of you is a key component to self-mastery.

Elements of Self-Mastery

- You and you alone are responsible for your internal state of being.
- Recover quickly. The past exists as long as you focus on it.
- Make a daily commitment to practice mastering self.
- Have fun learning the skills that lead to self-mastery. Invent new ways to respond to old issues.
- When you master SELF, mastering the world is EASY.

If I offered you heaven on Earth, would you be willing to make the commitment to self-mastery? Interestingly enough, some people are committed to self-mastery and some aren't. Some people are governed by circumstances and some are governed by other people. I choose neither one of those options, because I've already lived that way and I still remember how it felt. It was similar to riding a roller coaster with its repetitive ups and downs, and the ride never ended until I chose to master self!

Remember, mastering self, like any other new skill, requires practice, patience, and more importantly, commitment. Self-mastery involves consciously committing to a daily, moment-by-moment practice. Your hard work will pay off when you begin to discover heaven is on Earth.

**Your Opinion Is My Opinion—Peace
& Happiness at All Costs**

When I made the unwavering commitment to find out HOW to remain happy—regardless of my circumstances—

my personal perspectives changed. Because of my commitment to prioritize peace and happiness, I was forced to make conscious adjustments to my behavior. Why? Because 99.9% of the things I did and said did not align with my priority of wanting to be happy. When I made wanting to be happy my number-one priority, I was forced to change. And with that change, my life changed. On this journey to discover how to remain happy, I found that I needed to develop and create new tools and strategies to counteract anything that didn't match my new priority: happiness at all costs.

First, I had to acknowledge and accept the fact that my happiness depended on one person—me. With this knowledge, I felt a sense of empowerment. I no longer had to depend on anyone else for me to be happy. Maintaining my happiness was solely my responsibility. This new concept of knowing I was responsible for my own happiness brought an added bonus of peace because that meant if I wasn't happy, it was my fault. I must confess that the majority of my life was spent relying on others and or circumstances to make me happy. Now my happiness is my responsibility. And between you and me, I AM the most qualified person for the job.

While doing what was needed to maintain my own happiness, I discovered another huge but freeing responsibility: Not only am I responsible for maintaining my happiness, I'm also responsible for maintaining harmony in each and every one of my relationships! At first this was definitely a hard concept to accept and even harder to believe, but it's true. I'll admit I spent a couple of decades denying this fact. It was so easy for me to blame the other person for the conflicts and discord in my relationships. In fact, I conjured up endless reasons and even more excuses where I made sure the blame was theirs. *I can't be the ONLY reason for disharmony in my relationships... can I?* Can't I blame the other person for their participation in the friction and discord? As hard as I tried to blame others for their actions, words, and behaviors, it always circled back to me. Why? Because I was responsible for my happiness. It really didn't matter which relationships I encountered throughout the day, whether it be my parents, children, friends, co-workers, relatives, or even strangers: the responsibility of creating harmony in all of the aforementioned relationships fell squarely on my shoulders. If I want to experience harmonious relationships, it's my job to create and cultivate them.

Presently, if there's any friction of any kind in any of my relationships, I have no one to blame but myself. Ouch! Let me apologize in advance for sharing this shocking revelation, but there are no exceptions to this rule. There are no exceptions to the "Law of Relationship Harmony."

How Does the Law of Relationship Harmony Work?

First of all, let me share that my "Law of Relationship Harmony" (LRH) was created because of the conflicts in my real-life relationships. When I use the word *conflict,* I refer to ANY conversation or encounter that's not harmonious. I discovered a simple but unknown secret: Voicing my opinions and harmonious relationships don't mix. Especially with people who are not accepting of others. If you are accepting of all opinions, and you've eliminated judgment from your lifestyle, then this story is not for you.

What's Your Opinion?

Your opinion depends solely on your personal perspective. Since your experiences are unique to *you*, it is impossible for you to perceive anything exactly the way I would, or vice versa. It was, initially, difficult for me to grasp that simple concept. In fact, it took me decades to finally let go of arguing my point (whatever is was) while trying to convince someone to change their perspective and adopt mine. Little did I realize that every time I argued my opinion I subtracted from my happiness.

Since subtracting from my happiness was no longer an option for me, I was compelled to find a solution. I was forced to begin to accept our differences. Think of it like this: We all have a set of fingerprints and we are all as different as our fingerprints. When you begin to accept the differences between you and your fellow "cohabitants," your level or experience of happiness dramatically increases. I began listening to people, with different *ears*. Instead of spending valuable time arguing my point and trying to convince others that my opinion was the only one that mattered, I spent my time accepting other people's opinions, or rather, their right to have them. Notice that this does not mean I change my opinion. It just means that now I do not spend my time trying to convince others that my opinion is right.

Think about it. How many times have you been in an argument with someone and midway through they stopped and exclaimed, "Oh, my God, you are right! I did not know what I was thinking. Thank God you shared *your* opinion with me because I have been wrong all this time!" Has that ever happened to you? It never happened to me. I used to spend time trying to convince somebody else of what I thought, and then had to listen to what they thought, and then I would present my side again . . . and then they would offer a rebuttal. ARGH! I have literally spent decades campaigning for my opinion to be accepted as the world's opinion. Our differences are what make our glorious world go round. Practice accepting differences without disagreeing with them and your quality of life will improve.

My Past Exposed

Years ago I handed out opinions like I was handing out candy on Halloween. Everyone in my presence got served. I even voiced opinions about people I never personally met. Athletes, celebrities, politicians, spiritual teachers—name a person, and I had an opinion about them. Not only did I have an opinion about everyone and everything that happened on this planet, I took it one step further. Everyone who had the *pleasure* of meeting me was subject to listening to my opinions. All of my "hostages" had one thing in common: they all had ears.

Guilty or Not Guilty

In 1995, former American football player O. J. Simpson was charged with two counts of murder. The criminal trial lasted nine months and was held in Los Angeles, California—my *backyard*. This case has been described as the most publicized criminal trial in American history. When Simpson was on trial for double homicide, I was working nights. This left me with free time during the day to watch the entire nine-month trial. Yes, watching the O.J. Simpson trial became a non-paying part-time job. I was consumed with the case; and after the criminal trial ended, Simpson was tried for punitive damages in a civil court. There I was, again, glued to the television set. Unbelievably, watching both trials wasn't enough. I also listened to radio and television commentary after each day of hearings. Adding to my wealth of trial information, I even purchased books from famous criminal attorneys in the country. Both of the O. J. Simpson trials provided me with a smorgasbord of judgment and opinions. I had definite opinions and righteous judgment about whether or not Simpson was guilty. I openly discussed my opinions about the trial lawyers, the witnesses, the judge, the jurors, and even opinions about the murdered victims. You can believe that in 1995, I shared my opinions and judgments with anyone with ears.

And to top it off, I collected evidence to prove my opinion was "right."

Whether or not O. J. Simpson was guilty of double homicide is not the point here. It's taken me almost fifteen years to realize that voicing my opinion with anyone who did not share the same opinion was divisive. I intentionally segregated people based on whether or not they shared my opinion as to whether or not O. J. Simpson was guilty of double homicide. I actually *de-friended* people who did not agree with me. I ended relationships with people I'd known for years. Looking back, voicing my opinion created a lot of division in my life. And along with the energy of division, comes the energy of unhappiness.

I've spent most of my life and a lot of energy voicing and arguing my opinions and my reasons for them. But what are opinions? Opinions are a personal preference based on an individual's perspective. How can you disagree with a personal perspective? More importantly, as I mentioned earlier, have you ever engaged in a back-and-forth discussion (aka argument) and the other person suddenly stops and yells out, "Oh My God, you're RIGHT! What was I thinking?" Every single person I've argued with about whether or not O.J. Simpson was guilty NEVER changed their mind. Not once! Not one person changed their opinion based on a discussion I had with them no matter how much "evidence" I supplied to support my opinion.

What's been your experience? When two or more people discuss opposing opinions, it usually plays out like an endless back-and-forth exchange with the grand finale statement of, "I guess we're just going to have to agree to disagree." Think about it: when's the last time you've changed a cultivated opinion?

Look around. This world is obsessed with never-ending discussions about what happened, why it happened, what should have happened, what could happen, and what will happen. Opinions are what make talk radio and television multi-billion dollar businesses. You can't escape them.

What's My Opinion?

My opinion is that I AM responsible for supplying the dose of harmony in all of my relationships. All of them. And because of this, I'll sincerely and vehemently AGREE with any opinion you might have! Besides, everyone is entitled to believe their opinion is valid. Have you ever had an argument with someone who agreed with you? The answer is no. We only argue with people we disagree with. And with that said, your opinion is now my opinion. Say goodbye to arguing, disagreements, and conflicts, and say hello to peace and harmony.

Is O. J. Simpson guilty of double homicide? "That's what the evidence shows."

Is O. J. Simpson not guilty of double homicide? "That's what the evidence shows."

Again, since my number-one priority is to maintain harmony in all of my relationships at all costs, I have an obligation to create and maintain the harmony I seek. I admit that my ego gets hurt and feels neglected; however, that's a necessary side-effect to create harmonious relationships. Besides, I'm sure my ego will quickly find another project to attach itself to.

Let me be perfectly clear when I pose the idea of whether or not I should voice my opinion: I'm talking about my day-in, day-out life. What would happen in my personal life if I agreed with all opposing opinions? Nothing but a peaceful encounter. I'm still able to maintain my opinion; it's just that no one needs to know it. No one ever needs to know my opinion, especially if it creates division. Unless it's my job to voice an opinion, I will continue to agree with all opinions I meet. If voicing my opinion does not create a harmonious encounter, then why would I choose to voice it?

Democrats versus Republicans, and Happiness

When I was growing up, my father would instigate a political discussion of Democrats versus Republicans, usually around the dinner table. Republicans versus Democrats, good versus bad (no matching order intended)—I received a thorough brainwashing, for sure. I was conditioned to dislike anyone who wasn't affiliated with both my parents' choice of political parties. I'll admit that as a young adult, I fell for the indoctrination hook, line, and sinker. Before meeting a person, I developed an opinion about them based on which political party they belonged to. That's more evidence of how my opinion created division. Now that my priority is to sustain peace during all circumstances, it doesn't matter to me whether you are affiliated with the Republican Party, Democratic Party, Libertarian Party, Peace and Freedom Party, Constitution Party, Tea Party, or the Green Party—I agree with them all.

What draws out more opinions than a national presidential election? I can't think of anything else at this moment. I admit that during the 2008 presidential election, my opinion as to whom I was going to vote for was plastered on several billboards throughout the state. (Exaggerated here, to make the point) I let my opinion be known with a *mega-megaphone*. I also shared my opinion with willing and unwilling hostages. I even remember making phone calls to people who I knew were undecided! Yes . . . I know, I know, it's hard for me to believe also. But that is what's so great about change and growth. We all have the ability to make different choices whenever the old choices stop serving us. Did sharing my political opinion create any peace for me? The answer is NO. Sharing my opinion with *opposing parties* never added to my peace, harmony, or happiness.

In 2012, the United States held an election that could have or could not have resulted in Barak Obama's second term. Even though Obama won the election, the poles showed this country was strongly divided. For me, the election did not have the same *feel* as the 2008 election did. I was too wrapped up in wanting to be happy. Don't get me wrong, I planned on voting, and I had a clear idea of who I wanted in the White House; however, I was no longer compelled to voice my opinion. In 2012, it didn't matter who I voted for. What mattered to me was how to engage in daily election conversations that

I knew I would inevitably have. Why? Because I take public transportation to and from downtown Los Angeles every day. Because on a daily basis, I encounter station security, janitorial staff, bus drivers, and passengers. I work in an office that occupies 12 floors in a 28-floor building divided into north and south towers. I literally have 700+ co-workers. Along with co-workers, there are hundreds of other tenants occupying the same building, including CHP officers, private security, maintenance/janitorial staff, and cafeteria employees. When I enter the front door, I pass more than 10 security officers before I reach the lobby. I literally speak to at least 15 people before I even arrive at the elevators. In my free time (lol), I teach 4 to 5 exercise classes every week. My classes are usually filled with 25 to 40 students. I literally have contact with hundreds of people on a weekly basis.

My behavior had to change between the 2008 and 2012 elections. It had to change because I changed. I changed because my priorities changed. My priorities changed from feeding my ego to a desire to create peaceful, harmonious relationships everywhere I landed. Discussing, arguing, voicing my opinion to hear others vehemently disagree with me did not feel good anymore. In 2012, I had a dilemma: how was I going to interact with the hundreds of people I saw on a daily basis?

As usual, several months prior to the election, the candidates hosted televised debates. And the next day following the debates, there was no escaping the political conversations, especially with my reputation for being opinionated.

RealitySpirituality: The Truth About Happiness

I distinctly remember walking into my office building after a night of presidential debates. To my left was a female security officer wearing a "Vote for Obama" button. Our eyes locked and I gave her the universal "two-thumbs-up" sign. A few more feet into the building, was a small group of Romney supporters huddled in a circle. I locked eyes with one of the Romney supporters, and guess what I did? I flashed another universal "two-thumbs-up" sign. My behavior was simple and really easy, and more importantly, harmoniously peaceful. For months prior to the election, I mirrored everyone's opinions, without ever stating mine.

When asked in 2012, "Who're you voting for?" I responded with, "I'm voting for the same person you're voting for, of course." Anyone who asked me my opinion on the election, I would encourage them to discuss their opinion first. All I had to do was listen intently and nod my head up and down, listen intently and nod my head up and down again. My opinion was their opinion, as far as they knew; and with that there was peace and harmony in my world. I was happy. They were happy. Harmony reigned supreme.

Time has passed and I still have my opinions, but now they live in exile. You see, my priorities have changed. Today, my number-one priority is to be happy and to create harmonious relationships.

I Relapsed

I recently had a recurring conversation with my dear, sweet mother. The key word here is reoccurring. My mother loves to watch the morning, afternoon, evening, and weekly news. If the news is on, she's watching it. As you might guess, my personal preference now is to not watch the news. My mother knows this fact; however, it doesn't stop her from trying to engage me in conversations about what's happening in the news. A lot of times, people want to insist that what's important to them also be important to others. I know, because I've been guilty of this as well.

My dear mother insists, "You should know what's going on in the world." "You should know what's happening in your community." "How will you know what to wear if you don't listen to the weather report?" All valid points; however, I seem to manage a life without receiving a daily dose of murder, rape, child abuse, mass shootings, beheadings, global warming (now being called climate change instead), and war stories.

My dear well-meaning mother actually gets annoyed because I don't watch the news. The last time my mother ended the recurring lecture, I thought to myself, "What's wrong with me agreeing to watch the news?" It doesn't mean I have to watch it. Is it really that important for me to disagree with an eighty-four-year-old woman? After all, I've been disagreeing with her for years on countless topics, and what have I created? Certainly not harmony or peace. My mother does not share or accept my opinion regarding why I don't watch the news; and, in reality, why should she? You can be sure that the next time the topic of watching the news comes up I'm going to let my mother know that she's been right all along! What was I thinking? Why would I deprive myself of a daily dose of negativity and brutal images?

Yes, voicing my opinion has become unnecessary for me, because I've switched my priorities. Now, my only priority is to be happy. Happy at all costs.

- Global warming is a serious issue. I agree.
- Global warming has been created by Liberal politicians. I agree.
- The United States is a racist country. I agree.
- The United States has evolved into a country of equality for all. I agree.
- Marriage is a right, not a privilege, and should be guaranteed to all consenting adults. I agree.
- Marriage should only be between a man and a woman. I agree.
- The death penalty needs to be enforced in this country. I agree.
- The death penalty needs to be abolished in this country. I agree.
- Drugs should be illegal. I agree.
- Drugs should be legal. I agree.
- The top ten problems in this country are (fill in the blank). I agree.
- Did I watch the news today? "Morning, noon, and night."

My solution is simple, easy, and it works ... for me. By the way, if you don't agree with my opinion, I don't either.

A Dose of Irritation

I spent the majority of my life getting irritated with someone or something or my circumstances. Yes, I was raised in a family where the emotion of irritation was as important as breakfast. In my family, if you weren't bothered by your circumstances, something was seriously wrong. Just as important, if someone didn't say or do something to irritate you, the day would not have been complete. Looking back, if I had a dollar for every time I was irritated, I would have a steady stream of income and could retire today! It's interesting to look in the mirror and admit the truth: I thought getting irritated was as "normal" as the sun rising. I mean, I am human, so isn't the emotion of irritation normal? The answer is no. The emotion of irritation is a manmade creation and a manmade emotion. Yes, I had to *learn* to feel the emotion of irritation. I had to *learn* to become irritated with people, places, and circumstances.

I've been asking the Universe to assist me to rid myself of the emotion of irritation for almost a decade now and I'm finally seeing a light at the end of the tunnel. The journey has been slow; however, when I think about how decades of my life have been spent, I can easily understand why this vetting process takes time. I'm grateful, thought, because slowly but surely the Universe has been assisting me to lighten my load of what "bothers" me. What bothered me yesterday does not bother me today. What bothers me today will be gone tomorrow. Thank you, Universe, for answering my prayer.

Here Comes Da Judge

All judgments subtract from happiness. ~rln

Recently, I attended a public speaking event with approximately 250 people. The speakers, as well as the audience, were culturally and socially diverse. According to the program, there were 17 speakers listed—including me. I don't like admitting this, but as I listened to each speaker, I began judging them . . . *negatively* judging them. As a former Toastmaster, I judged them on their speech content and their delivery. Each speaker was allowed 4 to 5 minutes to talk, and as I judgmentally listened to each speaker, I began feeling worse and worse. My Universal antenna was screaming at me. Yes, yes, yes . . . I know that indulging in judgmental behavior subtracts from my happiness *and* I know that I'm a reflection of my judgments (ouch), but I couldn't stop it. I was on a runaway judgment train. Then, without fail, the Universe realized my dilemma and "They" decided to step in and dig me out of my downward spiral.

Universe to the Rescue

After approximately seven speakers presented, a professional comedian was brought on stage to offer some much needed and welcomed comic relief. I was pleasantly surprised because this comedian was hysterical. I laughed out loud the minute he cracked his first joke. What was so funny? He began making fun of the previous speakers and actually verbalized a few of my own negative judgments. Not only did he make fun of the speakers, he poked fun at the event itself. This guy had little reverence for the sophisticated social gathering as he dropped the "F" bomb more times than I could count. This made me laugh even harder. I verbally thanked the Universe for the welcomed *break* in the program. Laughter was exactly what I needed to snap me out of my judgmental fog. Besides, now I had someone else to do the "dirty work" for me. I was really enjoying his on-point observations, but then something happened to immediately stop me from laughing.

As I mentioned, there were people in attendance who had a variety of cultural, economic, and religious backgrounds. In fact, one of the first speakers that day was a flaming-out-of-the-closet-born-again Christian. I was sitting in the front row and Ms. Born Again was also sitting in the front row approximately five seats to my left. At first, I hadn't paid much attention to Ms. Born Again until her "Thank-you, Jesus" speech, which of course I negatively judged. Now, Ms. Born Again was sitting on the edge of her seat moving her head rapidly side to side with complete disapproval and disgust for the foul-mouthed politically-incorrect comedian. My focus shifted from having a great time to silence. Ms. Born Again looked like she was about to explode. She kept squirming in her seat while exhaling audible sighs. Now I was paying attention to her and how offended she was. As the comedian continued, Ms. Born Again began displaying even more noticeable disgust by covering her mouth with her hand, while her eyes opened wider and wider with each four-letter word spoken.

My attention went from enjoying the comedian to focusing on a narrow-minded, judgmental woman in the flesh. Hmm ... Something felt oddly familiar to me. (Remember, I'd been struggling with my own judgmental behavior prior to the comedian taking the stage.)

As I kept my eyes on Ms. Born Again, the Universe spoke directly to me: "That woman with her hand over her mouth, shaking her head in disapproval, is you," They announced. "What? No she's not," I shot back with a quick argument. At first, I refused to accept the Universe's obvious claim. "She's intolerant," I argued, and "I'm very tolerant." It was a losing battle. I was pleading my case to deaf ears, or rather, All Knowing Ears.

The Universe spoke to me again. "Whenever you judge someone else's behavior, including your own, you are intolerant—intolerant to someone else's preferences, intolerant to someone else's perspectives, and more importantly, intolerant to Self." That Universal bullet shot me right between the eyes. It was at that moment that I was able to actually see myself through another woman's behavior.

Thank you, Universe, for the visual; and, thank you for the lesson. Now, I get it.

CHAPTER 6

Happiness and Forgiveness

Forgiveness is one of the highest expressions of Love. Practice the art of forgiveness with Others and with Self because without it you cannot be happy. ~ rln

The subject of forgiveness is one of my favorite topics. Who has not been in a situation that requires forgiving someone? In my opinion, when you choose not to forgive and, more importantly, choose not to forgive *quickly*, you might as well drink a cup of poison every day of your life until you make the *selfish* choice to forgive.

Yes, true forgiveness is selfish. It seems odd to say, but when you choose to forgive, you are acting in your best interest. Of course, the other person benefits from your actions, or can; however, you are the person receiving the most benefit. When I finally realized that forgiveness has nothing to do with another person—that forgiveness is a gift that keeps on giving to Self, I was sold.

Let me share a few personal stories. While growing up I witnessed a lot of behaviors that taught me how I was supposed to act if I felt slighted or wronged, but immediate acts of forgiveness were not included. When my mother and father argued, their behavior was always followed by what I called "punishment." My father would give my mother the "cold shoulder" and not speak to her for days. Honestly, looking back, I can see why I did not know there were other choices I could have made. It was not until I met my now ex-husband that I learned that a couple was supposed to "talk out" their problems and "never go to bed angry." My husband might as well have been speaking a foreign language when he explained this to me. Not only did I find the concept of working problems out a problem in itself, but I believed that any type of compromise was a sign of weakness!

During my most impressionable years, I witnessed how my father and his only brother ostracized each other for over more than a decade. They'd had a falling-out over how to manage an apartment building they both owned. Over the years I have since realized the real problem was not how they needed to manage the apartment building, but how they managed their relationship. I believe that in most families, the real problems are unresolved issues that may have arisen during childhood.

I recall a grandmother who banished her son because of the woman he chose to marry. All of my life I have watched mothers, fathers, siblings, aunts, uncles, and cousins engage in "You're dead to me" behavior. So, it is understandable why I adopted the same types of social and relationship skills.

Yes, I admit that I have indulged in off-and-on relationships with people for years. Childhood friends, relatives, in-laws, co-workers, boyfriends, students—the list is quite extensive. I honestly did not know that (1) I could choose a different type of behavior than the one I learned early in my life, and (2) I was harming myself both physically and emotionally with my behaviors. Just like Dorothy in *The Wizard of Oz*, I had the power to create whatever type of relationship I wanted. But I did not know that . . . until now.

A year before my father died, my mother disinherited me for reasons she believed were just, and chose not to speak to or see me for years. At this point, I have not seen my mother in over five years, which I hope to change in the near future. Interestingly, even though I remain disinherited, we speak to each other nearly every day. I make it a point to end every conversation with a heartfelt, "I love you, Mommy!" Have you ever heard of a child who was disinherited and kept the lines of communication open with the parent who disinherited them? I have not.

It is really simple: If I choose to harbor bad feelings, I am choosing toxic behavior. I have never known toxic behavior to result in anything good. Have you?

Death and Forgiveness

I have been given permission to share a story from someone who is very special in my life. In 1991, my friend experienced an unbelievable tragedy. His story is a testament to happiness, death, personal growth, spiritual evolution, and forgiveness.

On July 11, 1991, two months after my friend married, his mother was killed by a drunk driver. She was driving home from work when her car was struck head-on. She didn't die instantly, so she suffered with open wounds until the emergency response team reached her more than twenty minutes later. I cannot image losing a loved one in that manner.

My friend was inconsolable. After that emotion wore off, he was after revenge. Coincidently, he was and still is a police officer and had access to more than one gun. Because he is a police officer, he also could enter the jail where the man who killed his mother was being held on the charge of manslaughter. When my friend, armed with a gun, arrived at the Los Angeles county jail, he was recognized by a fellow officer and, thank God, was refused entry into the facility. His plan for revenge was thwarted. He went through the motions and buried his mother three days after she was killed.

Twenty Years Later

My friend held onto the anger he felt for his mother's killer for twenty years. He also felt guilty during those twenty years because, as he explains, the last conversation he had with his mother was an argument over the telephone. He couldn't remember exactly what they'd argued about, but that didn't change how strong the guilt was that took over his life. Note: This is a great reminder to be grateful for loved ones in every moment because we never know if there will be any future moments.

My friend now has a different outlook about the events that unfolded that day. After twenty years he discovered new perspectives that have allowed him to feel good about what happened on that tragic day. *What?!* Yes, you heard me.

"For twenty years I had the opportunity to mourn, cry, and be sad; and I will admit that I was sad for what seemed like a lifetime. When I grew tired of grieving and feeling sad, I began to dig deep to search for a different way to feel. I wanted to find a different perspective that would make me feel good about my mother's death, our last conversation, and the man who took her life. Twenty years later, I have a new and improved outlook on life and death. Because of the way my mother died, I was given the opportunity to learn the importance of forgiveness. I learned that forgiveness was mandatory if I wanted to be happy. I learned that forgiveness started with forgiving myself for everything that I claimed responsibility for in my life. I forgave myself for feeling guilty about the last conversation I'd had with my mother. I forgave the man who killed my mother. And because I learned how to forgive, I can wish him good fortune in his life.

When my mother was alive, I never felt like I had an opportunity to be my own person. I was never able to be independent and stand alone. Now, for the first time in my life, I stand alone, without needing to be supported emotionally. After my mother died, I became an independent thinker. I became stronger emotionally. After my mother died, I was able to become more of myself.

Hurry Up, Mom

There was something else I needed to forgive myself for. Reflecting back on the relationship I had with my mother, there was one other thing I regretted: Not having patience with her. I regretted rushing her, especially when she was eating. My mother ate extremely slowly. Whenever we went out to eat, I made comments about just how slow she was. But despite my nagging her to eat faster, she never did. There is a McDonald's on the corner of Redondo Boulevard & Figueroa Street in Los Angeles, California, where my mother and I often frequented. She would order the same meal every time: a fish filet sandwich, French fries, and a soda. I remember being impatient with her every time we sat down. Why did she eat so slowly? It would literally take her five bites to finish one French fry! It was maddening. I can't tell you how many times I let her know how unhappy I was with the amount of time it took her to finish a meal.

On January 22, 2014, I drove back to the neighborhood where I grew up. I drove to that same McDonald's my mother and I used to visit at least once a week for almost ten years. I ordered exactly what my mother used to order. I felt my mother's spirit as I sat down to eat. I wished her a happy birthday before I started because on that day she would have been seventy-six years old. I began to eat my fries just as slowly as my mother *would have eaten them—one teeny-tiny bite at a time, a small bite of the sandwich, another small sip of soda. One more tiny bite of a fry and then a teeny-weeny sip of soda.*

On my mother's birthday, I purposely spent two hours finishing my meal. During that time I forgave myself for being impatient with my mother while she was alive. It took twenty years and my mother's death to be the person I am today. Finally, I am at peace with all that this life brings." ~ *C.E.C.*

Forgive as Quickly as Possible

For most people a decision to forgive comes, if ever, at the end of a long emotional journey that may stretch over months, if not years. I will admit, for the majority of my life, forgiving was not on my "things to do" list. When I found out the truth about the benefits of forgiveness, I began practicing the skill immediately. I was able to forgive my mother years before she was able to forgive me, because when you do not actively practice the skill of forgiveness, you are not able to forgive quickly. Like any other skill, if you do not practice it on a regular basis, you get rusty. When you are rusty, you lose the ability to make different choices as easily as you might.

I practice forgiveness on a daily basis. Yes, I am committed to keeping that skill-set high. After all, I have been blessed with countless people I had to forgive at one time or another. It took me a while to believe, without any doubt, the overwhelming evidence that forgiveness is a required ingredient of true happiness. If you want inner peace and contentment, or just to grow as a person, you must master this skill. Mastering the skill of forgiveness takes you to another level of spirituality.

Whether you believe Jesus was the son of God or whether you believe Jesus did not exist, you cannot ignore the story of the biggest example of forgiveness that has ever been told. While alive, Jesus taught forgiveness. During his last hours of life, Jesus *was* forgiveness. I am sure you recognize this important quote from the Bible: "Father, forgive them, for they know not what they do."

Have you ever thought about how powerful that statement really is? Can you imagine how anyone, man or woman, has the ability in the moment, while nailed to a cross, being tortured, mocked, and slowly and unmercifully executed, to utter those words—and mean them? An act of forgiveness at such a crucial moment seems impossible to comprehend; however, without forgiveness, you have sentenced yourself to an internal prison.

How to Forgive Instantly

Since I have learned the skill of forgiveness the hard way, I have learned several facts. I have also discovered strategies that will aid you on your quest to be able to forgive anyone for anything.

Five Facts about Forgiveness

- You make a choice to forgive.

- You make a choice not to forgive.
- You cannot pick and choose which behaviors to forgive. ALL circumstances fall under the heading of forgiveness.
- Forgiveness is Health Food for Your Soul.
- Forgiveness does not require words. Forgiveness is an actual energy that you emit.

When You Are Challenged

When you are given opportunities to forgive, remember this: Whatever has happened, never take a "slight" personally. This is a really tough concept, but one that is necessary to grasp. Think back to the story of my own experience with the aggressive driver. How many times have you been angry because of how someone else drove in traffic? It is easy to get angry with someone who just cut you off in traffic; however, there is more than one way to interpret the same incident, whether it matches the facts or not, facts which you may never know. As I mentioned previously, maybe the driver had received a phone call informing him that a loved one was just rushed to the hospital. Would you be forgiving of his driving behaviors if you knew those were the circumstances? I know I would.

Let us say your forgiveness skills are at best rusty, or at worst non-existent. There is hope. Remember, you will not be able to pick and choose your circumstances, but you will be able to choose a different behavior than what you are used to.

On February 21, 2013, I was in New York City. It was my son's twenty-eighth birthday. While he worked I decided to visit the 9/11 Memorial. I was in awe of the surroundings. From my perspective the site exuded peace, growth, and the resilience of man. Before my eyes I witnessed the undeniable Universal Law of Cause and Effect. There is never a cause without an effect or an effect without a cause. Is it possible to forgive nineteen terrorists who brought death and destruction to thousands on that day? Only YOU can answer that question. What I do know is this: whether you choose to practice forgiveness or whether you choose not to practice forgiveness, you will be choosing how you will somehow, someway, be immediately affected.

Forgive Yourself

We think about forgiveness as something we give to others; however, we often forget to afford the same courtesy to ourselves. In fact, the ability to forgive one's self is essential in order to be able to forgive another. I would like to share some of the things I needed to forgive myself for.

- I forgive myself for not trusting the Divine Order of the Universe.
- I forgive myself for not listening to and acting on my own intuition.
- I forgive myself for not acknowledging my own worth.
- I forgive myself for wanting to be what I am not.

- I forgive myself for settling for and accepting less than what I am worth.
- I forgive myself for not loving myself unconditionally.
- I forgive myself for being impatient with myself and others.
- I forgive myself for thinking I've wasted time.
- I forgive myself for resisting moments.
- I forgive myself for getting angry with myself and others.
- I forgive myself for intentionally being mean to myself and others.
- I forgive myself for disliking any part of my physical appearance.
- I forgive myself for blaming others for the problems in my life.
- I forgive myself for focusing on what's wrong instead of what's right.
- I forgive myself for thinking my value depended on my bank account.
- I forgive myself for thinking my value depended on a title and accomplishments.
- I forgive myself for following the rules, regulations, and expectations of society.
- I forgive myself for thinking my way is the best way.
- I forgive myself for judging others and judging myself.
- I forgive myself for not feeling the present moment is enough.
- I forgive myself for wanting anything other that what I am experiencing.

- I forgive myself for thinking I could have been a better mother.
- I forgive myself for not being myself.
- I forgive myself for not being able to forgive myself.
- I forgive myself for doubting my innate Divinity.

What about you? Make a list of things you haven't been able to forgive yourself for then read them out loud three times. Increase your energy with each reading so that the last time you read them you are literally screaming out loud. Then, burn the list. You're done. It's over. Next moment.

CHAPTER 7

Death and Happiness

Death is inevitable. How you react to death is a choice. ~rln

This is going to sound CraZy, but the day I buried my father was one of the happiest days of my life. Before I clarify why, I need to explain that I was taught *how* to perceive and respond to death. Yes, I learned *how* to perceive death—as sad, and I learned *how* to respond to death—as tragic. I was conditioned to respond like the majority of people in the United States respond to death. How about you? How do you respond when you hear about someone's death? Here are a few standard responses.

- I'm so sorry for your loss.
- I'll pray for you.
- I'm here for you if you need anything.
- My heart goes out to you during this difficult time.
- That's so sad (et cetera).

Let me be clear. All of the above responses are well intended and appropriate. However, I don't want to respond, think, or react like the masses. I want to perceive death differently than the majority in the U.S., and I want to respond to death differently than the majority of people respond to death. My response to death is as unique as I am. And that's why the day my father was buried was a celebrated, memorable, and happy day.

Now, before I could feel happy on the day my father was buried, I had to be de-briefed, de-bugged, and de-brainwashed. Happiness had been a priority of mine for decades prior to my father's actual death, and I was committed to being happy, regardless of the circumstances. Why was I so committed and focused on changing my thoughts about death? It's really easy to explain: I had an only-child to raise.

How do you teach your child about death? More specifically, how do I teach my only son that he has choices as to how to respond to my eventual death? It was a question that, as he got older, I needed an answer to.

Back Story

Like most of us, I've attended several funerals in my lifetime. There was one in particular that I'll never forget. In 2003, a friend of mine had been diagnosed with breast cancer. She was aggressively treated with radiation and chemotherapy and eventually went into remission. A couple of years later the cancer returned, and again she was treated with radiation and chemotherapy. This time the cancer won. After my friend realized her eventual fate, it took approximately eight months before she finally died.

The service was held in a newly constructed public library in an extremely wealthy, prominent city. My girlfriend had held the position of head librarian; therefore, the location of the service was more than appropriate. She was an extraordinarily intelligent woman who was known for her character, as well as her courage. She left behind a husband and her only child, a daughter, who was in her early twenties. Of course, the girl experienced almost a decade of watching her mother's ongoing battle with cancer, including witnessing the effects of the debilitating treatments that followed. I can't imagine how traumatic, as well as emotionally draining this was for the young girl, along with experiencing her mother's slow death.

On the day of the funeral, this poor girl wept and screamed uncontrollably throughout the entire service. Her father tried to console his daughter without any success. Visibly, she was an emotional wreck. Her pain on that day tore at my heart while also leaving a lasting impression. It was obvious there was nothing anyone could do or say that would help this girl feel different about her mother's death.

My thoughts went immediately to my only child, Nathan. It was on that day that I made up my mind that I did not want my son to experience my death in the same manner as this young woman experienced her mother's. I did not want my son to experience my loss with a collection of pre-set emotional conditions. I wanted my son to have multiple options and choices as to how to feel. I did not want my son to "fall apart," because that's all he was taught to do. I knew there must be other ways to express and experience the loss of a parent without being overwhelmed with feelings of total despair, grief, and sadness—unless that's how you want to feel. There had to be other choices as to how respond to the death of a loved one.

Note: I don't like admitting this, but it's the truth. This experience happened during a time in my life when I was really into blaming other people for things that happened. I distinctly remember being angry and blaming both of her parents for not preparing their only child for this inevitable day. It wasn't as if her mother's death came as a surprise. I know now that this girl experienced exactly what she needed to experience in exactly the way she needed to experience it. No, her parents were not to blame for her emotional response. But you couldn't have convinced me of that truth then.

My History

When I was in my twenties and thirties, I definitely related to that young girl and how she must have felt. Reflecting back, it would hurt my heart when I imagined my life without either of my parents. I even remember saying to myself, "If my mother or father died, I don't know what I'd do." I was, excuse the pun, "dead serious." I didn't know it then, but I was stuck on only one way of thinking. Why was I stuck on only one perspective? I believe the reason why I kept that limited perspective was due to societal conditioning, along with watching too many movies. Yes, when I was younger, a conversation about my parents dying would've been too painful for me to bear. I spent many years avoiding the emotional fall-out from death, until the day I witnessed my friend's daughter in so much pain. I'm deeply grateful to her because her behavior inspired me to want to be and behave a different way.

Ask and It Is Given

I didn't know how it was going to happen, but as a mother, I wanted something different for my son. I definitely needed help with this assignment. I needed to ask the Universe, and I did: "Universe, how do I teach my son a different way to view and respond to death; and, more specifically, a different way to respond to my death?"

Fortunately, when I ask the Universe for help, I'm always given an answer. Five years had passed since I'd witnessed my friend's daughter suffering such emotional pain due to the death of her mother. And five years had passed since I'd asked the Universe for help. Finally, on July 2, 2008, the day I buried my father, the Universe gave me my answer.

At the time of my father's death, my perspective of death had changed. I was no longer fearful of dying, and I never avoided discussing the topic with my son. Why? On the day my father was buried I knew the following:

- We are all energy, and energy cannot be created or destroyed.
- Energy never dies.
- There are societies that actually celebrate death, and I wanted to embrace that way of thinking instead of how I was taught.

Ralph Norrington, My Father

My memories and photographs became priceless after my father died. This is one of the first pictures I have with my father, Ralph Norrington. This picture represents the beginning of our relationship.

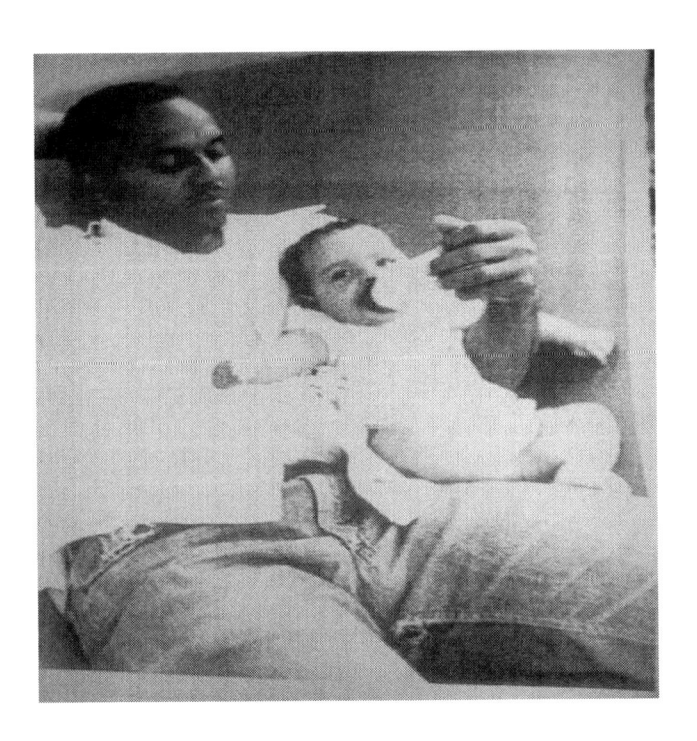

My father was a smart, progressive man. He was strong both mentally and physically. In my eyes, he was invincible. He was my Superman, and I was Daddy's little girl—truly, his favorite. His passions? He had one: My father was passionate about making money.

He took this next picture in 1965. It was his first investment, an apartment building with 100 units located in Chicago, Illinois, where he grew up.

My father was a closet entertainer, as well. He loved to sing and tell jokes. From Sinatra to Stevie Wonder... my dad sang all the classics. He was never without a joke to share either, whether you wanted to hear it or not.

As you can probably imagine, my father taught me a lot of lessons during the time I shared his eighty-four years of life. Some of them include:

"Your life is your responsibility."
"Be a leader NOT a follower."
"If you lend out money don't expect to get it back."

And my favorite . . .

"Don't call boys, let them call you."

RealitySpirituality: The Truth About Happiness

In 2002, my dad, my Superman, was diagnosed with *hydrocephalus*. It's a disease that parallels Alzheimer's. In my opinion, this disease was a gift from the Universe. You see, this illness stripped my father of every wall he'd spent a lifetime building around his heart. When I was a child, even though my father adored me, I never heard the words, "I love you;" and I don't remember my father hugging or kissing me once.

One day, while I was chauffeuring him to his adult daycare center, I stretched out my right hand to him. My father, my Superman, grabbed it and didn't let go. I drove the entire distance with my left hand holding the steering wheel and my right hand tightly gripping his, while buckets of tears streamed down my cheeks. Not one word was spoken during the fifteen-minute drive.

While growing up, my father often told me what I was doing wrong; but because of this disease, the only words I heard from him were praise.

"You're the greatest, girl."
"I'm so proud of you."
"You're so smart."

His encouraging words and compliments where never-ending. Every time I'd visit my father he'd shower me with more such words. It didn't take me long to realize it, but the Universe gifted me with five years with the father I'd always wanted.

In January 2007, my father was admitted into a hospice facility. Superman was down to 114 pounds, and his doctors gave him two weeks to live. I knew this was going to be my last visit with him, and on this day, I said good-bye.

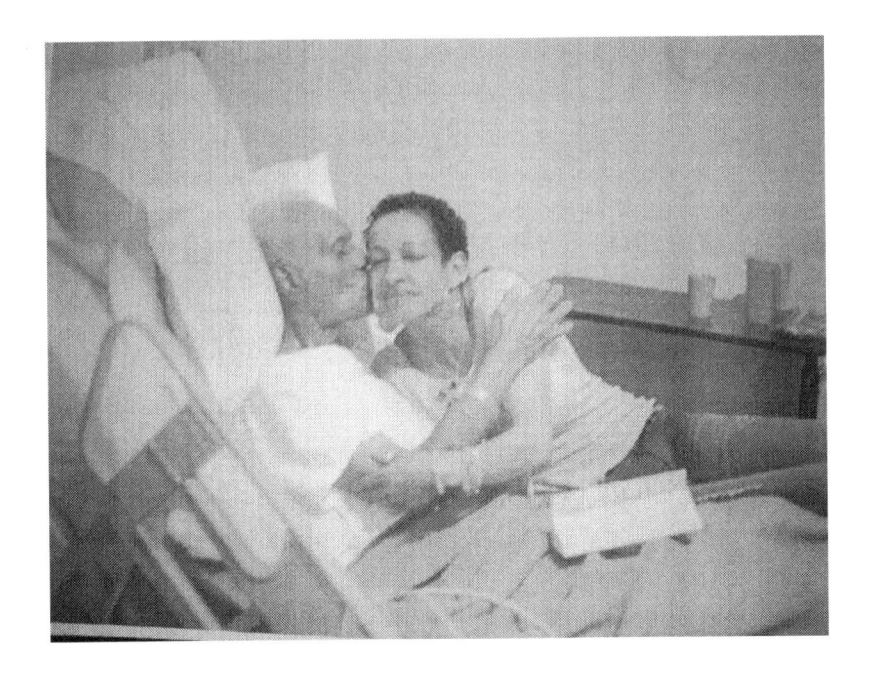

Well, two weeks turned in two months, and two months turned into a year-and-a-half. Ralph Norrington, my Superman, was kicked out of hospice for refusing to die! The reason? I believe there were more lessons my father wanted to teach his only daughter.

The last year and a half of my father's life was spent in a convalescent home. He was confined to a wheelchair, while dependent on a team of medical staff and caregivers to take care of him, and yet, he never complained.

RealitySpirituality: The Truth About Happiness

The Lesson: Complaining is a choice.

I remember spending hours outside with my father, seated next to him while we watched cars drive by.

The Lesson: It doesn't matter how you spend time—as long as you remain grateful for every moment.

My father never lost the ability to make me laugh. When I'd tell him I loved him, he would reply, "*Nooow* you tell me."

The Lesson: Laughter IS the best medicine.

My father greeted everyone with a smile. He was never in a bad mood ... well ... unless my mother was around. (JK) Hey, even Superman had his kryptonite.

My father also taught me this during the last eighteen months of his life:

The Lesson: Singing out loud is always appropriate.

The Lesson: Money has nothing to do with how happy your life is.

And my favorite...

The Lesson: If you want mayonnaise on your hamburger, you don't have to open the bun!

RealitySpirituality: The Truth About Happiness

On Saturday, June 21, 2008, I called my father and heard his voice for the last time. It was low and weak but he managed to say, "Hi, Sugar." All I could think to say was, "I love you, Daddy. I love you. I love you. I love you." And he replied, "I love you, too."

He died two days later.

My father's death was a gift from the Universe. The question I had asked five years earlier was about to be answered.

It was a hot, bright, beautiful day in July. The service was held at 1:00 P.M. My son, Nathan, flew in from Lovell, Maine, where he was working summer stock theatre. *Coincidentally*, the day of my father's funeral service just happened to fall on my son's only day off from work. Otherwise, according to his supervisor, he would not have been able to attend. Nathan purchased a same-day roundtrip ticket and was flying back to Maine that evening. Steve-O, my ex-husband, also attended my father's funeral services. As it happened, I'd reconciled with him three months prior to my father's death. We had not spoken to each other for almost seven years due to more than one court proceeding. My small intimate family of three was united on July 2, 2008.

At the service, I spoke for about twenty-five minutes, sharing the influences my father had on me and my life. Yes, I shed tears while I spoke; and yes, I was emotional. But my emotions did not come from a place of grief, sadness, or despair. The tears flowed because I was sharing, with all who listened, my fondest memories. I also spoke about the many lessons I'd learned from my father and the influence he'd had on my life. I spoke about how during those last five years, our roles eventually reversed.

On July 2, 2008, I was the living example my son needed to witness. How do you respond to the death of a parent? Watch me Nathan. Watch the Universe work through me.

After the service, Nathan and I had a few hours before his plane was scheduled to depart. We made a couple of pit stops, changed clothes at a local gas station on the route, and began driving in the direction of Los Angeles International Airport (LAX). We had a few hours to spare, so I chose to drive past the airport. We landed at Playa del Ray Beach, where I'd spent a lot of time as a child. I grabbed a couple of beach towels from the trunk of my car and we hiked down a steep hill. We found a perfect spot close to the water and sat on our towels in silence, while looking out at the Pacific Ocean.

Finally, Nathan asked me, "Mom, how do you feel? How do you really feel now that Gramps is dead?" At that moment I felt my father's presence and I smiled. In fact, I couldn't stop smiling. My father's body was no longer here, but I could feel his presence. I could even feel his light, playful energy. In honor of my father, I made a joke out of the question: "What?" I looked at my son with a surprised face and said, "Gramps is dead?" My son looked at me as though he hadn't heard me correctly. Why was I smiling? Why wasn't I sad? Why wasn't I feeling bad? At first my son didn't understand how I could be so happy on the day I buried my father, but after a few seconds, he got it.

How was I able to switch perspectives on July 2, 2008?

- I remained focused on feeling grateful for my father's life and my role in it.
- I could not be grateful and sad at the same time. I chose to be grateful.
- I was conscious that my son was watching me closely, and I wanted to give him a memory he'd never forget.
- The Universe granted me a perfect opportunity to be the example my son needed for his future journey.
- My father was sitting next to me, cheering.

My son and I laughed and laughed and laughed some more. We hugged each and acknowledged this was a perfect day to remember. Then, we did what we always do, which we memorialized with a photograph of that moment. This picture was taken on July 2, 2008, one hour after I buried my father.

The Lesson: Finally, it was my turn to teach my son how to LIVE after I die.

What Pancake Taught Me

"A-O Pangay" ~rln

It was Christmas 1993. My son was eight years old when my ex-husband and I surprised him with his first dog—Pancake. Pancake was available for adoption when she was eight weeks old. We were one of eight families that wanted her. Three eights: 8-8-8? You could say that all of the stars were in alignment for us to get her. I just *knew* she was going to be a part of our family regardless of how many other people wanted her. Sure enough, the Universe agreed; and on December 23, 1993, we won the Pancake lottery.

Back Story

Even though my husband and I divorced when our son was two years old, we still celebrated all of the holidays together as a family. Christmas was one of our favorites. My ex-husband would drive over to my house early Christmas morning and we'd watch our son open his gifts from "Santa Claus." In 1993, the most significant gift was not found under the Christmas tree. Pancake was outside in the backyard waiting to be discovered. I wish I had a video that captured the moment my son saw his best friend for the next sixteen years. It was a truly priceless experience.

After what seemed like an eternity of playing outside with (at the time) a nameless puppy, it was time for our traditional Christmas breakfast which was—you guessed it—pancakes. Looking back, it was comical that the three of us spent a whole lot of time trying to think of appropriate names for our newest family member when the answer was literally right under our noses. The *light bulb* finally went on when we reverted to using physical descriptions for names that would fit. Pancake was golden brown, like a pancake, and the rest is history.

During the sixteen years of Pancake's life with us, she taught each of us countless Universal lessons. I'd like to share a few of my favorites.

It might sound strange, but as I evolved as a person, Pancake evolved as a dog. When we first brought her home from the shelter, she was afraid of her own shadow. I used to joke that she had low self-esteem, but in reality Pancake was really a reflection of me. As I grew, Pancake grew. During her sixteen years, she grew confident in her own fur. She found freedom from oppression. She shed being afraid. She discovered who she was. She was honest about what she wanted and refused to take no for an answer. She was the boss of her life and she refused to be influenced or led by anyone, including me. As you can imagine, Pancake taught me a lot in those years. Finally, one year before she died, she taught me (1) how to say no with love, (2) how not to take anything personally, (3) how to communicate without emotion, and (4) how not to judge.

I'm old-fashioned when it comes to hair care. After I wash my hair, I roll it with huge pink, green, and yellow rollers. I own an original beauty shop hair drying *helmet* that is attached to a chair. This piece of *furniture* sits in my garage to this day. Depending on the length of my hair, it usually takes twenty to thirty minutes for it to completely dry after it's been washed and rolled.

When I'd sit in the garage drying my hair, I spent most of the time petting Pancake. When she was younger, she couldn't get enough of me petting her. If I stopped petting her, she would push her nose under my hand or would nudge me or wiggle her way under my leg. She wasn't too proud to beg for affection.

During the last couple years of her life, she changed. I'd still sit under the dryer and pet her; but now, when Pancake had enough affection, she would walk away from me. It was really interesting because I never understood why she would walk away *while* I was petting her. I made the analogy of it being like ending a massage before it was over. Why would she walk away from me when I was in the middle of showing her love and affection? It was a question I never got an answer to.

When Pancake had had enough affection and began to walk away, I'd tap my hand on the chair and call her back. Every time I'd call her, she'd turn her head and look at me as if to say, "I love you, but no thank you." Then she would turn around and start walking away. I would always try to call her back; but when she was ready to leave, that was it, and she'd disappear to wherever she preferred to be in that moment.

Lessons

- Pancake taught me how to communicate calmly and without emotion.
- Pancake taught me how to not take anything personally.
- Pancake taught me how to accept her without judgments.
- Pancake taught me how to say no with love.

The last years of Pancake's life was filled with more love and acceptance than ever.

In 2006, my son moved to New York, and Pancake became my sole responsibility. Our relationship shifted, and Pancake and I grew closer. One hot summer day, while I was walking her, without warning, Pancake had a seizure. I watched in horror as her body began to violently convulse over and over again. She fell to the ground. I'd never experienced anything like it before and, admittedly, I was frozen in shock for a couple of seconds. When her head hit the pavement, I instinctively picked her up and held her in my arms. I held her until the seizure ended. It seemed like forever, but in reality it was just a few minutes. Miraculously, after the episode ended, Pancake resumed being herself, as though nothing unusual had happened. All animals live in the moment, and that traumatic-for-me moment was over, as far as she was concerned. That day I realized Pancake was in the last stage of her life. I cried the rest of the way home while holding her in my arms. As far as I know, Pancake did not have another seizure other than the one I witnessed that day.

Thank God Pancake's decline did not happen overnight. I didn't know it then but I was going to be given two more years with her, and most of those days were spent in appreciation for this dog that loved so unconditionally. During those last two years of her life, she lost most of her hearing and some of her eyesight. Even with the losses, she was full of life and endless love. During her last few months, she developed a chronic cough. I took her to a veterinarian, who wanted to perform surgery. I refused. I didn't stop searching until I found a doctor I felt an energy connection with. He told me the reason Pancake was coughing was because there was fluid in her lungs. He prescribed medication, and for a few months, her coughing stabilized. Then there came the day when Pancake refused to take her medication, even though I camouflaged the pills in peanut butter, chicken, bacon, steak, and bologna. Soon after Pancake refused her meds, she refused to eat.

It was a Friday afternoon when Pancake and I took what I thought was going to be our final trip to the veterinarian. She usually sat in the back seat, but on this trip I let her sit next to me, in the passenger's seat. As I drove, I watched her as she enjoyed one of her favorite things to do while riding in an automobile—stick her head out of the window. She was so adorable, and precious. It was almost too much for me to bear.

I explained to the veterinarian that Pancake was not taking her meds, was not eating, and was barely drinking. To my relief and total surprise, the doctor offered me a brief bit of solace. He told me to continue to observe her over the weekend, and if nothing changed, I was to bring her back on Monday to put her down. He also shared a personal story that helped me with my decision. He told me that one of the biggest regrets in his life was keeping his own dog alive too long; that his dog suffered longer than necessary because of his own selfishness; and that if he had the chance to "do it all over again," he would have ended his dog's suffering earlier than later. I'd never had to make the decision to put a dog to *sleep*. And even though Pancake was family, I consciously wanted what was best for her.

I spent the last two days of Pancake's life celebrating her life. But Monday came much too quickly. While getting dressed, I thought about *how* I could represent my son's presence on Pancake's last day. I went to his bedroom closet and grabbed a mustard-colored polo shirt that still had my son's scent on it. I immediately put it on, along with the darkest pair of sunglasses I owned. Then, Pancake and I went to the veterinarian's office for the very last time.

I don't remember a lot of the specifics, but I do remember holding her the entire time: Her feet never touched the ground. We were immediately escorted into a waiting room—and we waited—we waited for Pancake's destiny to unfold. When the doctor came into the room, he explained the procedure in detail and what I was to expect afterward. Then he shaved a small spot on her body. He then asked me if I wanted to be alone with her. Of course I said yes. I don't remember all my words, but I do remember repeating over and over again how much I loved her. I told her how many people loved her and I thanked her for everything she did to contribute to my own life. Finally, I called for the doctor to proceed with the inevitable. I held Pancake in my arms until she stopped breathing.

Looking back, I wish I could have held her tighter and I wish I hadn't cried as much as I did. But knowing Pancake as I did, she was okay with it all. I love you, Pancake.

CHAPTER 8

How to Live in the Moment

Before I discuss how to live in the moment, I'd like to say that living in the moment is, in reality, our true nature. Yes, we were all born experiencing only the present moment. Interestingly enough, we continued living in the present moment until we were approximately four or five years old. It's really crazy that we've evolved into living in the past and or future, rather than what was naturally intended.

Have you ever spent time watching a toddler experience life? A toddler hasn't been indoctrinated with the infinite amount of adult thinking—yet. No, you won't hear a three-year-old repeating any of the following statements like mantras, the way adults tend to.

- I'm not worthy.
- I don't like the way I look.
- I don't have enough money.
- I'm too fat.

- I'm too old.
- I'm too short.
- I'm not smart enough.
- I'm worried.
- I'm afraid.
- I'm a failure.

Programmed at Birth

We've all been programmed and conditioned at an early age, to label, blame, judge, compare, label, blame, judge, compare, and repeat and repeat this. We've also been programmed and conditioned to live in the past, as well as the future, or even more unsettling, in our own heads. However, when we choose to indulge in this type of behavior, we automatically give up the gift of living in the present moment. Why? Because, when you label a circumstance, event, or person "good" or "bad," you're using a reference from the past. You cannot use a reference from the past and be in the present moment at the same time.

Are Our Thoughts the Enemy?

No. Our thoughts are just that—thoughts. It's only when we pay attention to *then* believe our thoughts are as real as the circumstances they refer to—and then take them seriously—that we suffer. Our thoughts about our circumstances (not the circumstances themselves) are responsible for ALL of our suffering. Our runaway, all-consuming thoughts are not evidence of the TRUTH. Our thoughts are evidence of our conditioning.

If our true nature is to live in the present moment, how do we live in that state of being that is enjoyed by children and the animal kingdom? How do we deprogram ourselves and live in the present moment?

Tip No. 1

Have the intention to live in the present moment every day! Repeat out loud:

"I intend to live in the moment more and more each day."

"I'm grateful I can experience living in the present moment throughout my day."

"How would it feel to experience living in the present moment all the time?" (*Ask and It Is Given* by Abraham-Hicks)

Tip No. 2

Commit to a daily habit of developing and practicing your awareness. I call this living consciously in an unconscious world. Yes, for the most part, we are unconscious creatures of habit; however, habitual behavior does not produce change or growth. Make a decision to change three habitual behaviors each week. Example: Drive home using a different route each day; or if you pack a lunch, eat out; or comb your hair in a different style; or think of three different (nice) responses you can make to a rude cashier. Have fun, and come up with your own personal changes. Challenge yourself and be creative. The point is to shake it up and practice doing things differently. There is no progress without practice.

Tip No. 3

In 2011, I voluntarily took a forty-day vow of silence. Now, I'm not suggesting that you do the same; however, I am suggesting that you spend some time throughout your day being quiet. And to be perfectly clear, I mean remaining quiet while surrounded by people. This practice will definitely heighten your awareness tenfold. The more awareness you have, the more present moments you will experience. Another benefit of this exercise is that when you practice silence, you become a better listener. When you *really listen* to someone, you're automatically in the present moment.

What's so Great about Living in the Moment?

Good question. The present moment is the only real reality we have. Anything other than the present moment is, in actuality, non-existent. The past doesn't exist unless we choose to think about it, and the future doesn't exist, period. The present moment is the only place we are able to make choices. The present moment is the foundation of our future moments. The present moment is where we'll find ultimate peace and contentment. The present moment silences the mind's chatter. In the present moment, time does not exist. The present moment is where the Universe resides.

CHAPTER 9

The Bitter Pill of Dissatisfaction

The more you are in harmony with yourself the more you are in harmony with the world. ~rln

I am always changing and evolving. During this stage in my life, I'm rapidly shedding behaviors, thoughts, and responses (or reactions) that don't serve my intention to sustain an inner foundation of happiness regardless of my outer circumstances. This shedding of worn-out, destructive behavior is a welcome change from how I used to live. Honestly, *I was emotionally worn out.* I needed to make a shift in order to find the peace of mind I longed for. It's really very simple: when my priorities changed, my life changed. Over a period of time, I chose to make my inner well-being the only focus of my attention.

Recently, I experienced an ongoing feeling that has challenged me for decades. This feeling does not mix well with my present daily focus of maintaining well-being (aka happiness). This feeling is the feeling of dissatisfaction. I don't know about you, but I've lived most of my adult life feeling dissatisfied with one thing or another. Yes, it was time to feel a different feeling and shed the lousy feeling of dissatisfaction once and for all.

Have you ever thought about where the feeling of dissatisfaction originated? We were not born with the concept of it. We were not born with this destructive (and in my opinion) useless emotion. No . . . We were all "fortunate" enough to learn, accept, and embrace this cancerous feeling of dissatisfaction as "normal." I could spend a week listing ALL the things I can remember feeling dissatisfied with and about. What about you? I compiled a short list below, in no particular order, of what I used to feel dissatisfied about.

Weight – Looks – Bank Account – Getting Older – Time – Circumstances – Job – Co-workers – Marriage – Divorce – Mother and or Father – All relatives – Boyfriends – Girlfriends – Husband (Sorry Steve-O) – Birthdays – Holidays – Traffic – Weather – Vacations – Fitness Level – Responses (from other people) – Haircut (yes, I said haircut) . . . blah, blah, blah!

Earlier in the book, I discuss the Law of Attraction. I'd like to remind you, again, that the Law of Attraction is actively working at all times, regardless of whether or not you believe it does or believe in it. When I began to really understand and accept the Law of Attraction as an undeniable force, I was compelled to make necessary changes in my life. You will continue to attract *more* reasons to be dissatisfied, until you stop and change your perspective about what is really happening in your life.

Can Satisfaction Be Guaranteed?

Look in the mirror and ask yourself: Do you like and accept what you have or is your attention focused on what you don't have? How do you feel about YOU today? Can you look in the mirror and feel a sense of pride and satisfaction in what you see? Can you feel satisfied with who you are? Can you feel satisfied with what you have accomplished? Is it even possible to feel satisfied about everything in your life? I say YES! And now I will share how.

The higher your level of awareness is the more likely you'll feel satisfied with who you are, where you are, your circumstances, and your experiences. Yes, my friends, feeling satisfied is an inside job. No amount of money or external things can bring you the internal feeling of the satisfaction you seek. Satisfaction begins and ends inside of you.

How Can You Raise Your Level of Awareness?

I'm glad you asked. There are several ways to raise your level of awareness, and I will share a few of my favorites.

- Know, without a doubt, that you are not alone. In every moment of your life, you have access to an energy force that creates worlds! You are the physical extension of that energy force. And you are just as powerful.

- Whenever you feel "out of whack," ask the Universe for guidance and then breathe and RELAX. When you ask it is always given. (Note: I'm not talking about asking for things, I'm talking about asking the Universe for peace *in* mind.) When your priority is peace of mind, there's nothing that will have the ability to shake your world. Nothing. Make a commitment to be different than you have been.

- Announce, out loud, that your heart is open and willing to accept all that is given. As your mind, heart, and body become more open, you will begin to feel different. You will begin to know what it's like to live in an open, flowing state of being, instead of living in an unconscious state of old habits and patterns.

- Announce, out loud, that you love your life! Accept all experiences and accept that the Universe does not make mistakes—regardless of how anything *appears.*

- Ask the Universe to keep you focused on the present moment, and release the rest. Begin to focus on your marvelous, spectacular daily journey, and not on the outcome.

- Love is patient and love is kind. Learn to be patient and kind with yourself. Become your own best friend.

Remember, whatever you've learned, you can unlearn.

"There are two ways of being rich. One is to have all you want, the other is to be satisfied and in love with what you have." ~Unknown

CHAPTER 10

Money and Happiness

*"The number-one drug in the civilized world is not heroine, cocaine, crystal meth, ecstasy, alcohol, painkillers, nicotine, caffeine, or sleeping medications. The number one drug in the civilized world is **money**. If you don't have money, you don't feel good. And when you do have money, you can never have enough. Some will do anything to get money, including selling their souls. There never seems to be an end to wanting more money. Think about it. Have you ever heard someone say 'No thank you, I don't want anymore money, I have enough?' I have never heard, met, or read about the condition of 'having enough money.' What I have been conditioned to think is that I will never have enough."* ~C.E.C.

I've spent the majority of my life wanting to have and or make more money. I can't remember a time when I was satisfied with the amount of money I had, even though I've never been without food, shelter, or clothing. I have a stable job that also provides medical and dental insurance. I own a home and an automobile, and I usually travel a couple of times each year to an out-of-state destination. Regardless of all of the above-mentioned abundances, I never felt as though I had enough money.

What I believe and experience as true is that the energy of *needing* anything does not flow with the order of the Universe. The energies and thoughts of lack and dissatisfaction do not align with Universal Energy. And when you are not aligned with Universal Energy, it's impossible to be happy. Money is a form of energy just as everything else is in this Universe. However, money or the lack of money itself does not have the power to make me unhappy—unless I make that choice.

Background

I remember my mother and father having endless conversations about money. Even though both parents worked full-time, there *seemed* to never be enough of the stuff. My family was always on some sort of budget. Whenever we were on a family outing (including our yearly vacation), I was always told how much everything cost. My mother shopped at three separate grocery stores in order to find the lowest food prices. My father, who was literally and figuratively in charge of our household, was a thrifty man. He did not enjoy spending money and complained about every penny spent. My beliefs about money formed at an early age, thanks to a Christmas day event that left me traumatized, in a particular way, for years.

As stated, my father "enjoyed" complaining about the cost of (you name it), including Christmas trees. Because of the "exorbitant" expense of a Christmas tree, he'd wait until

Christmas Eve to purchase the family tree, when the cost of trees would significantly decease. In 1968, when I was thirteen, the cost of a Christmas tree on Christmas Eve was twenty dollars. According to my father, this was highway robbery. He refused to purchase our family tree that year. Apparently, a tree wasn't that important and certainly not worth the twenty dollars to make his family happy. I remember leaving the tree lot in total shock and disbelief that for the first time in my life, I would not have a Christmas tree on Christmas day. I just knew my father was going to surprise us all; that we'd wake up Christmas morning with a tree that would have magically appeared, just as the Christmas gifts had magically appeared under the tree every year since I became aware of them at three years old. Certainly, my father wasn't going to allow money to ruin his only daughter's Christmas, was he? It turned out that's exactly what happened.

On Christmas morning I ran down the stairs to a living room without a tree or gifts. I was more than disappointed, I was literally in shock. My shock morphed into depression. I did not know it then, but I would spend the rest of my unconscious days (pre-awakened state-of-being days that is) with deep-rooted negative judgments about cheap people. I was actually offended by anyone (male or female) who displayed behavior that was the opposite of generous. But I digress.

Money = Success?

I was taught that *I* was the reason I didn't have an endless supply of money. And there are countless books, programs, seminars, retreats, and inspirational leaders that continue to teach that same philosophy. I was also taught that money equals success. I believe the majority of people believe money and success are interchangeable: "If I don't have a lot of money, how can I be considered successful?" I bought into that mindset *for years*. In fact, someone I highly respected told me having money meant having freedom, and that having a lot of money meant I could do more good deeds. But are those two statements true? I discovered that neither one of them is true. Freedom is a state of mind.

My Money Chakra Is Blocked

I also used to buy into the ridiculous concept that I was "blocking" money from me; that I created my own lack. No wonder I was unhappy. Now, I don't believe I've ever blocked money from myself. And I don't believe that I can think, visualize, pray for, or recite affirmations to obtain money. What I do believe is that when it's my time to experience a never-ending amount of money, I will. And for whatever reason I'm not experiencing money *growing on trees* in this lifetime, there's always another zillion lifetimes when that can be my experience.

Further, the Law of Abundance says that we have more than enough to meet our needs. When we have Universal balance with money, we have total trust that whatever we need will be provided. We are not afraid to spend money on ourselves or use it to help others. The money itself is not the issue. We do whatever we are here to do, knowing that the resources (money, people, and circumstances) will flow to us ... and through us.

What I Thought about Money Was the Problem

In 2012, I discovered that the reason I felt dissatisfied had nothing to do with how much money I did or didn't have. I learned that money itself was not real problem. The real problem was my thoughts *about* money. Why did I think I lacked something because I didn't have money—at the moment? The value I placed on money was a huge challenge I needed to confront. The good news is that since I had *learned* to place that level of value on money; I could also unlearn what was making me unhappy about that. My beliefs about money needed an overhaul. Even my judgments about cheap people needed to change. I was obligated to change, because no matter how much money I have or don't have, happiness will always remain my number-one priority. And because happiness is my number-one priority, I was compelled to establish other ways to think about money.

I've since discovered that lack of money has *never* been the reason why I've been unhappy. It had nothing to do with the amount of money I had in the bank. I was under the illusion that lack of money determined my unhappiness, but I was completely wrong.

Think about it. There are existing cultures that survive off the land. Cultures that hunt for their daily food, and literally live in rustic homes more open to the air, moon, and sun than most of us live in. If I brought them a thousand dollar bill and told them it was valuable, I would be considered insane. Reflecting back, it's hard to believe I placed a value on *myself* based on a series of numbers. For years, my self-worth was determined by a piece of paper with manmade symbols and designs.

Cheap people are people, too; though, previously, I never met a cheap person I didn't try to change. What's interesting about that is I was the one who needed to change. (Feel free to substitute the word *cheap* for any *type* of person you don't get along with.) Know this: it's never them. It's always you.

A New Perspective

When your perspective shifts, your life will shift too. When you change your attitude and feelings toward money, you will begin to make a gradual inner shift about worth and value. Something really happens. Something really changes. How do you change your relationship with money? Change your perspective, and you change your relationship with money.

Can you envision feeling at peace regardless of how much money you have?

Can you envision feeling powerful and worthy regardless of how much money you have?

RealitySpirituality: The Truth About Happiness

Are you able to be happy regardless of how much money you have?

Finally, after forty years, my answers to these questions are a resounding YES.

Remember, you don't need money to

- Feel good about yourself
- Do good
- Experience freedom
- Be of service to others
- Smile
- Be kind
- Be patient
- Live in the moment
- Eliminate judgments, comparisons, anger, dissatisfaction, fear, worry, and sadness
- Flow with reality
- Be grateful for what you have
- Be satisfied
- Be Happy

CHAPTER 11

Holidays and Happiness

This chapter does not focus on the religious meaning behind the holidays. My focus in this chapter is to share my thoughts as to WHY some people feel blue, sad, depressed, and lonely on or around the holidays. ~rln

I'll never forget the day my son, who was sixteen at the time, said, "Mom, holidays are overrated!" My son's comment was a truly important one. Why? Because to him holidays felt overrated. At the time, I didn't understand or even agree with his comment, but now I can say that I get it.

What I'm about to share with you is from my own experience and perspective. I do not pretend to have the answers as to why some people feel depressed, lonely, or sad during the holidays. What I can do is share what the holidays mean to me now and how I changed the way I celebrate them.

How can the season of merriment, joyfulness, festiveness, happiness, and warmth create so much depression, sadness, and loneliness? In my opinion, one of the main reasons is having enormous expectations. Expecting the day to unfold without a glitch. Expecting to be surrounded by loved ones who behave perfectly. Expecting the day to unfold on a timely schedule. Expecting to give and receive the perfect gift. Expecting magic. Expecting an illusion.

Back Story

I was brought up in a home where holidays like Christmas, Easter, Thanksgiving, New Year's Day, Fourth of July, along with my own birthday, were celebrated on a large "Super Bowl" day scale. Yes, my birthdays and holidays were more than just another day. Those "anointed" days became events filled with growing expectations. So, not only did I have huge expectations for the day, I spent an inordinate amount of time preparing for the day.

Prior to each birthday and holiday, I'd purchase new clothes, new shoes, and even new undies. My hair and make-up had to be picture-perfect, too. And the gifts—oh, the gifts! I spent a lot of time shopping for gifts with anticipation and high expectations of pleasing someone else! And, if the person I gave the gift to didn't respond in a manner that I thought was honestly happy and grateful, my day was literally ruined.

As I grew older, my expectations of the *anointed* days also grew. *Houston, we have a problem.* Preparing for any holiday actually taught me how to maintain extensive expectations. Preparing for any holiday also taught me how to NOT live in the present moment. When I look back and think about all of the expectations I had prior to the actual day, it's no wonder I stopped enjoying the holidays as I had once done as a child. For me, holidays became an obligation instead of a celebration. There was too much pressure—too much pressure to enjoy the day.

In 2006, my son left for college in New York City. It was only then that my perception of what a holiday should feel like to me changed. For me, the change came when I discovered that all expectations lead to unhappiness. As I've stated, being happy is a priority for me. When I began eliminating expectations, I literally became happier. Along with eliminating expectations, I began to feel better about spending time alone. I would have never felt good about spending a holiday alone, until I felt good about being alone.

Shortly after I began feeling good about being alone, I also began to shift my perception about "special" occasions, including holidays. Let's think about it. There are 7.2 billion people living on this planet. Are you telling me that on a particular day, I'm supposed to celebrate the way other people choose to celebrate? Who wrote these holiday rules for me to follow? What if I don't want to celebrate the holidays the way the masses celebrate the holidays? Why do I have to talk to or hang out with family on a specific day? If I don't, does that mean I don't love them? No, it does not. It means that I am living and doing on that day what I'm inspired to do—not what I've been told I'm "obligated" to do, by virtue of someone's rules. It means that I'm living in the moment, and living in the moment means that I don't know how I'm going to feel on any particular day, including the holiday, until that day is here.

"The one who follows the crowd will usually get no further than the crowd. The one who walks alone is likely to find himself in places no one has ever been." ~ Albert Einstein

What if I want to spend the holiday meditating? Or, what if I want to spend the holiday hiking or exercising—by myself? Or, what if I want to spend the holiday reading, watching a movie, or writing an article about what a fabulous day I'm having? What about that?! If I don't want to hang out with family or friends, am I supposed to feel bad about it? Not any more. You might argue that my loved ones will be disappointed if I choose to exclude them on such an important day. Honestly, if you claim to love me, then you will love what makes me feel connected to the Universe.

Is It Possible to Be Single and Happy on Valentine's Day?

February 14 is Valentine's Day in the United States, and love is in the air: you can't escape it. It's a day to celebrate being and falling in love. But what if you don't have that special person in your life on Valentine's Day? Is it possible to be happy on Valentine's Day, even when you're single? I say, emphatically, YES, and I would like to share five ways to be happy on Valentine's Day, especially when you're single.

RealitySpirituality: The Truth About Happiness

1. This is a perfect day to focus on you. Use the day to fall in love with You. The truth is the more you exhibit love for yourself the more you open yourself up to love from another and others. Just as you would plan a date with a special someone, plan to treat yourself to things you love to do. Buy yourself flowers. Get a massage. Dine in or take out from your favorite restaurant. Watch your favorite movie and or listen to your favorite music.

2. Cheer someone else up. Volunteer your services at a convalescent home, a children's hospital, or a Veteran's hospital. Purchase Valentine's Day cards in bulk, sign them, and hand them out to perfect strangers throughout the day. Contact people whom you haven't spoken with in awhile. Make it your intention to be the reason someone else smiles on Valentine's Day.

3. Create a list of ten things you are grateful for. There is no substitute for expressing gratitude. You cannot be grateful and depressed at the same time.

4. Change your perspective. There are several ways you can immediately change your perspective so that you feel good being alone on Valentine's Day. Example: Instead of thinking you are spending the day alone, change your perspective to reflect a celebratory day of meditation.

5. Face it, there are several reasons to celebrate being single. Most of our greatest moments of self-improvement, insights, and periods of growth occur while spending time alone.

What Are You Doing for the Holidays?

I don't know about you, but the majority of people I know spend a lot of time asking each other, "What are you going to do for the holidays?" Before my newfound freedom, I used to make stuff up because I wasn't convicted in my convictions.

Now, when anyone asks me what I'm doing for Christmas, New Year's Eve, Thanksgiving, et cetera, I state with renewed conviction, "Absolutely nothing," if that's what I've chosen to do. I usually hear said (out of concern), "Would you like to come to my house?" "No thank you," I respond lovingly. "I'm spending the day alone"... again. People always look confused because I have a huge smile on my face, and I then add, "I'm looking forward to the day." The idea that I should be with family or friends and or attend a ritual function is a manmade concept.

Finally, after all these decades, I've eliminated the pressure and expectations that the holidays used to mean. Yes, holidays are special; however, they're no more special than any other day in my life. That's why I celebrate each day, every twenty-four hours.

My New Year's Resolution for 2014

How many of you made New Year's resolutions for 2014? Are there things you'd like to accomplish in this year (or whichever year you're reading this in)? Are there goals you'd like to achieve? I used to write down several things I wanted to accomplish, at the beginning of each year. Resolutions like lose weight, exercise more, eat healthier, accomplish more, make more money . . . blah, blah, blah. I also used to write down and visualize what I wanted to manifest that year. At this point in my life, I have given up wanting and desiring anything. Let me explain. I have two priorities in my life: one is to live to my potential and the other is to be happy.

I define "living to my potential" as growing and evolving as a person. I am proud to say that I am and have been evolving with each day that passes. Yes, I am a different person today than I was yesterday. People who know me know this to be true. I used to be a bitch-on-wheels. It was my way or the highway. I was very opinionated, and my opinions were always right. I was quick to anger and I never, ever backed down from a fight. Arguments and conflicts were daily pastimes of mine. If you disagreed with me, something was wrong with *you* and I let you know it. I held grudges forever. I was a big fan of getting revenge. I was dissatisfied with myself and my life. I was quick to judge myself and even quicker to judge others. I was critical of myself and others. I complained about anything and everything. The bottom line is this: I was miserable. How *could* I be happy when I lived and exhibited those types of behaviors?

Recently, my son, Nathan, asked me, "Mom, what can you tell me that you've learned in your life that I might not know?" After years of seeking and finding foundational components to happiness, this is what I told him: "The most important thing in my life is my daily moment-by-moment connection with the Universe."

What does that mean? It means that my connection with the Universe is my sole priority (my priority to be happy is a sub-priority of my sole priority because my happiness is dependent on my connection with the Universe). Why is living connected to the Universe my sole priority? Because I've spent countless years living disconnected, and I know the difference. Living connected to the Universe means that whatever crosses my path in this lifetime, I am at peace. Living connected to the Universe means that I am content and happy with ALL that happens and ALL that doesn't happen.

When I live *disconnected* to the Universe, I experience emotions like sadness, irritation, anger, resentment, fear, frustration, jealously, envy, and impatience . . . just to name a few. To add insult to injury, accompanying those emotions are behaviors such as complaining, judging, comparing, blaming, worrying, nervousness, tension—all while focusing on what's wrong. Let me be clear: I am not saying that any of those emotions or behaviors is bad. What I am saying is that I'd rather experience other emotions and exhibit other types of behavior. And since I have a choice (you do too), I'd rather experience emotions that feel good to me. I'd rather exhibit behaviors such as acceptance, unconditional love, happiness, patience, non-resistance, forgiveness, and tolerance that will add to the well-being of this amazing global community.

Therefore, my only, and I repeat, my ONLY resolution in 2014, is to engage in daily practices of strengthening my connection to the Universe. What about you?

CHAPTER 12

Be the Change You Want to See in the World

Change your perspective, change your Life, change the world. ~rln

I don't know where Einstein received his inspiration, but my inspiration often reveals itself in the shower. The shower is where I meditate and enjoy conversations with the Universe. Currently, I practice developing new perspectives about old issues. Anytime I feel something is amiss in my personal energy force-field, it's time to change my perspective. Developing the ability to change your perspective, when "this thing called life" challenges you, is extremely important to sustain inner peace and happiness. And, easily enough, when we practice daily, our perspectives can be changed in an instant. The speed of our thoughts is instantaneous and infinite.

In 2013, I made plans to attend my first book release party on Long Island, in the state of New York. I'd never been to Long Island, and I was excited about the experience. My mother was also excited and began studying the Long Island weather reports a week prior to my trip in June. My mother loves watching The Weather Channel. I'm not sure how long she watches each day. I do know that this woman can provide a daily weather report for any state in the country.

A week before I left for the East Coast, my mother called me with the weather report. According to my mother, Long Island was expecting heavy rainstorms during my visit. My mother was worried (probably due to the recent storms the East Coast had experienced). You might say she was annoyingly concerned. Yes, I become annoyed when my mother fears for my safety. Why? Because I don't live my life worried and in a state of constant fear, and I expect my mother to think and behave like I do!

Note: My mother has always been one of my biggest challenges. I know, however, that the role she plays in my life is vitally important for my own personal and spiritual growth.

The day I was scheduled to depart from Burbank, California, was June 9, 2013. My mother called with her most recent weather report. "Becky, it's going to rain while you're there. Make sure to pack an umbrella," she ordered. Now, I don't know about you, but the day I leave on an extended trip, I'm usually juggling several things at once while, in addition, watching the clock. This day was no different. I spent that day packing clothes, unpacking clothes, packing make-up, hair products, shoes, PJs, toothbrush, ID, travel purse—checking and double-checking to make sure I'd packed everything I'd need on the trip. On that day of my departure, I was feeling anxious energy. It wasn't a good time for weatherwoman

Wilma to call and insist I add an extra item to my already over-packed suitcase.

At first, I tried to blame my irritated mood on my mother. Then, of course, the Universe reminded me it's impossible to blame my agitated state on the actions of another. Thanks again, Universe, for the timely reminder.

Back to the story. Instead of me responding lovingly with a simple "All right, Mom" when she told me to pack an umbrella, my mother heard silence on the other end of the line. I was silent because I know myself and I know what I really wanted to say was, "Shut the (insert strong expletive here) up. I'm fifty years old; and if I want to bring an umbrella on this trip, I will. I don't need packing instructions and unnecessary worry from my mommy."

Much to my chagrin, my mother didn't accept the silence. She asked me a second time, "Do you have a fold-up umbrella you can pack in your suitcase?" I tried giving her the "silent treatment" again, with no luck. *Argh!* The Universe is so (expletive) persistent. Now my mother is asking me if I can hear her. "Yes, I heard you, Mom," I said, without responding to her (expletive) question. At this point, the steam was steadily rising in my body and I could feel it blowing out of my ears. "*Beeeecky*, do you have a fold-up umbrella you can pack?" she repeated for the third time. The third time was a "charm" for me—and I lost it. "Mom," I barked, "I'm not bringing an umbrella with me; and if I need an umbrella, I can always buy an umbrella. Further, if I'm outside and it's raining, I won't be outside for long; and besides, it's just water!" Of course, I immediately felt like crap for losing my patience with her and surrendering my peaceful energy. I say "peaceful." Yes, I had anxious excitement, but I didn't want anything extra added to it. I remember mumbling an un-heartfelt apology.

A few days after the incident, I shared this story with my son. The genius that he is said, "You know, Mom, she only offers you suggestions because she cares so much about you." Ouch! Who asked him for advice? Weren't children meant to be seen and not heard?

When you think something is going wrong in your life, you have three ways to respond. You can (1) complain—to yourself or others; (2) blame—yourself or others; or (3) change—yourself. If life doesn't go according to your plan or your expectations, how do YOU respond? I'm asking this because I used to spend a lot of my valuable time and energy complaining and blaming without a thought of what I was creating for my future moments. Admittedly, I didn't know I had other options, but now that I know I can change my thoughts and my behavior, I'm on board.

When I used to complain, guess what I discovered? I never had a shortage of circumstances or people to complain about. Never. The complaint "well" never ran dry. Yes, I was able to complain at any given time, 24/7, 365 days a year. The supply of complaints was endless. What's even worse—and laughable—is that I thought complaining was "normal." Look around, or more importantly, look in the mirror. I don't know too many people who don't complain on a daily basis. You?

Don't think for a minute that complaining was the only thing on my "to-do" list. No, I also liked to blame everybody and anybody (but myself) for my unhappiness. Oh, I loved that one. Take responsibility for my unhappiness? No thank you. Especially when there're *so* many other people to blame. Right?

It was only when I consciously made happiness my number-one priority that I made the decision to change my behavior. Why is it So Important to Change? Earlier in the book, I talked about the Universal Law of Cause and Effect. The Law of Cause and Effect states that for every action, there is an equal reaction. This is extremely important because WHATEVER action (cause) you emit, you will receive a corresponding reaction (effect). And, by the way, it doesn't matter whether or not you believe in the validity of the Universal Laws. Whatever you cause, you will experience an equal effect. There are no exceptions to the Laws of the Universe. None. Ninguno. Aucun. Méiyǒu. Keine.

The Solution

When I started to accept that everything, and I mean EVERYTHING, that happened to me was actually a blessing and or a valuable lesson, I changed my thoughts. I also changed my reactions to all circumstances. When I changed my thoughts and my reactions, I automatically changed my behavior. I began asking, "How is this experience serving me?" As I started to look for the good in the otherwise "bad" situation, my focus changed from finding what's wrong to discovering what's right! It may sound cRaZy, but it works for me. Without question, I'm much happier now.

Great things flow effortlessly to all who are accountable for their actions. I encourage you, my dear friends, to take accountability to the next level. When you realize you have the power and the ability to change your behavior, life gets easier, and you will smile, inside and out, a lot more. An added bonus: When YOU change, the world changes!

360 Ways to Be Happy

You can change your perspective in an instant. ~rln

There are 360 degrees in a circle. Each degree represents a different perspective. I contend that there are 360 ways or 360 different perspectives in every moment to choose to be happy. We are constantly making decisions (whether consciously or unconsciously) to be happy or unhappy in every moment we experience. If there is a moment that is making you unhappy, all you have to do is change your perspective until you find a perspective that *will* make you happy.

Example: A woman called in to my radio show and told me she had just started a new job. At first she was excited about her new position, but soon her happiness turned to discontent because of the one-and-a-half-hour commute she was now facing twice a day. Even though she had just been hired, she seriously considered quitting because of the added gas expense and the long drive.

I asked her if she could possibly think of another perspective for her exact same situation that would allow her to feel good about the long drive. In other words, was she able to find happiness within something she was unhappy about?

She paused for awhile, and to her credit thought of three separate perspectives that actually shifted her energy from discontentment to contentment. Here's what she said.

- I have one and a half hours to be alone with the Universe.
- I can contact people I don't usually have time to talk to.
- I can share with others how to change their perspective if they're ever unhappy in the moment.

Isn't that amazing?! I contend that when you practice changing perspectives, your life also changes. And you will be happier; I don't care how dire the situation is. In any given moment, you have 360 different perspectives that will enable you to smile about what you thought made you unhappy. Practice changing your perspective the next time you feel unhappy. Remember, a perspective can be changed in an instant.

I Am at Peace

Living connected to the Universe is the only way to *be* at peace. Because the Universe *is* peace, the Universe is always at peace. When you live *connected* to the Universe, regardless of what happens, you feel only peace. When you connect to the Universe, it's impossible to feel irritated, disturbed, annoyed, angry, worried, anxious, sad, hurt, offended, unsatisfied, moody, jealous, or (fill in the blank).

- Living connected to the Universe means that whatever anyone says to me, I am at peace.
- Living connected to the Universe means that if I have health issues, I am at peace.
- Living connected to the Universe means that if I'm broke, I am at peace.
- Living connected to the Universe means that if I am homeless, I am at peace.
- Living connected to the Universe means that whatever happens to me, I am at peace.
- Living connected to the Universe means that whatever doesn't happen to me, I am at peace.

Universe, What Did You Say?

One of my most important discoveries is to acknowledge my direct communication with the Universe. I do not claim to be unique. I believe all of us have the ability to communicate with Source at anytime, for any reason. It doesn't matter who you are or the circumstances for which you require answers: everyone is heard and everyone is answered. In order for me to hear what the Universe is saying, I must be

- Open to receive
- Committed
- Still and quiet

Open to receive: I spent a lot of my adult life with an impenetrable, closed mind. I knew everything and I knew I knew everything. However, there came a time when I outgrew the misery. My "way" didn't work anymore. Figuratively, I kept hitting brick walls. I *needed* a change. No outsiders could have intervened and quickened my journey. I had to reach a point where I needed to travel on another path. This is what I mean when I say you have to be open to receive. When you are open to receive, you are open to change. When you are open to receive, you will be able to hear and then listen to a new voice.

Committed: Commitment to change is like jumping off a cliff every morning you wake up. Yes, I had to make a commitment to jump off the cliff each day. And, in reality, that's exactly how it feels. However, the more you jump the easier it gets. The more you jump the more the fear goes away. And the less fear you have the more you want to jump. When you make it your daily habit to jump off the proverbial cliff, you guarantee that one day it will feel like you're flying. And then you will spend the rest of your life's journey flying on the wings of the Universe.

Be still, be quiet: The Universe is always communicating with us. All we have to do is quiet ourselves and listen. It seems like that would be easy to do, but believe me, it's not. I used to be extremely uncomfortable with silence. I needed some type of noise to keep me company. It was impossible for me to sit quietly without reading, listening to music, or watching television. How about you? Are you able to sit alone quietly long enough to watch the sunset? As I mentioned earlier, in

2011, I took a forty-day vow of silence, and that experience changed me forever. I was extremely uncomfortable during the first week, but after that I enjoyed the freedom of not having to speak. (If necessary, I did communicate through text and e-mails). For forty days I relied on my personal energy to communicate with others, which entailed listening, hand gestures, and a lot of smiling. It also was a great test of self-awareness. Anytime you want answers, be still and be quiet.

Universe, Why?

I used to ask the Universe why: Why did (fill in the blank) happen to me? If you ever find yourself asking *why*, maybe I can help you with that. I've listed a few reasons why things *happen* to us. Feel free to choose one or all of the answers below, whenever you feel the need to ask "Why me?"

Why Me?
- Because whatever happens is for my betterment
- Because whatever happens is for my evolution and growth
- Because whatever happens is in Divine order
- Because whatever happens is necessary for my journey
- Because whatever happens is not personal
- Because whatever happens is not serious
- Because whatever happens is supposed to happen
- Because whatever happens has been planned since the beginning of time

RealitySpirituality: The Truth About Happiness

- Because it's all part of a bigger plan
- Because I needed it
- Because I now have an opportunity to find the good in whatever happened
- Because the Universe doesn't make mistakes
- Because the Universe loves me
- Because I AM the Universe

CHAPTER 13

Ask Rebecca Anything!

The following questions are from real people, with real challenges, asking for my counsel. My answers are written to (1) find the truth and then (2) assist them with finding peace and happiness.

Dear Rebecca,

You talk about sustaining happiness no matter what your circumstances are. How is that possible?

Signed,

Anonymous

Dear Anonymous,

First of all, happiness is more than a feeling! Real happiness is a state of being that cannot be taken or shaken without your permission. Learning how to sustain happiness, no matter what the circumstances, is a highly-developed skill that takes years (yes, I said years) of commitment and practice.

Think about it: Michael Jordan didn't become the world's best basketball player overnight.

Prioritize Happiness. Merely wanting to be happy is not enough. You must want to be happy with the same intensity and fervor you have as a need to breathe. In reality, sustaining happiness is a never-ending 24/7, 365 days a year, full-time job. The compelling results, however, are worth the commitment. Who doesn't want heaven on Earth?

Practice. Practice behaviors that add to your happiness and eliminate behaviors that don't. Sounds simple enough, but more often that not, we consciously or unconsciously find ourselves engaging in daily behaviors that actually SUBTRACT from our happiness! Can you name behaviors and thoughts that add to your happiness? Can you name behaviors and thoughts that subtract from your happiness? That is the first step: to recognize which behaviors and thoughts add or subtract from your happiness.

Patience. Be patient with yourself. New behaviors and new thoughts take time to integrate into your life. It took time to develop into who you are now, and it will take time to develop into who you will become. You'll find that your journey will mirror the moves of the queen in a chess match: forward, backwards, diagonal, and sideways. The exciting news is that every move will be considered progress.

Love is patient. Love is kind. Be patient with yourself. Be your own best friend.

Love,

Rebecca

RealitySpirituality: The Truth About Happiness

Dear Rebecca,

I've been experiencing an extreme amount of anxiety lately and I would like your input. Recently, my husband and I purchased our first home. A few days after purchasing the house, we discovered an ant infestation and faulty plumbing, all while hosting my new in-laws. I'm someone who experiences major anxiety, and the above circumstance literally took me out. Can you please share some techniques that will help me cope with anxiety in the future? I need suggestions to counter the anxiety.

Thank you,
Anonymous

Thank you, Anonymous, for the great question. And thank you for your willingness to share your personal story.

First of all, I'd like you to close your eyes, take a deep breath, and use your creativity to describe yourself differently. You described yourself as "someone who experiences major anxiety." I would like you to find new labels to describe who you really are.

Example: I'm someone who is challenged from time to time, and so far I've survived every one of my challenges with fortitude, courage, and guidance from the Universe.

Second, we can only experience one emotion at a time. And you have the ability and the power to change any unwanted emotion at any time—especially if the emotion isn't serving your best interests. Admittedly, this is not necessarily easy and the process takes time, practice, and patience, but I guarantee you, it's worth developing this new skill.

Example: You can choose the emotion of feeling anxious or choose the emotion of feeling grateful. Grateful that you are able to own your own home!

Do you realize there are people who would trade places with you and your husband in a New York minute? I know a few people who would LOVE to own their own home, even with (expletive here) infestation of ants, plumbing problems, gutted bathrooms, and in-laws who don't have the sense to stay in a hotel down the street! Further, I'd like to remind you that all of the "challenges" that you're fortunate enough to experience will also change. Nothing ever stays the same.

How to Relieve Anxiety While in the Moment

- Physically, take yourself OUT of the situation for a bit. Go to the park, walk around the block, take a drive, sing a song, dance a jig, go to the movies, get a massage, listen to music that you love. Trust me: Your circumstances will still be waiting for you when you get back home. I call this technique resetting your thermostat. When you find yourself not feeling the way you'd like to feel, you need to ACTIVELY reset your thermostat. Also, the resetting of your personal thermostat works best if you are alone.

- Breathe, breathe, breathe. Most of us breathe throughout our day using shallow breaths. Try not to wait until you're in crisis mode to breathe more deeply. On a daily basis, practice breathing deeper and slower. When you are consciously taking deeper and longer breaths, the tension in your body automatically relaxes.

- Can you find something to laugh about in the middle of your anxiety attack? Try to take yourself out of thinking "Everything is going wrong" to "This experience could be a number-one rated sitcom!" *Where's my pen?* Journal your experience as if you were going to audition for NBC. Hey, *Seinfeld*'s off the air (not really); we need another number-one rated comedy show. We need YOUR story! I guarantee you'll be able to laugh about your present "disaster" in the future. The trick is to discover that you CAN laugh about any circumstance while in the moment. This creative way of thinking also takes practice and patience before you're *hot under the collar*.

- Know that you're always actively creating your future moments and experiences. It's really important to remain mindful of this fact, especially when you are in the midst of an emotional storm.

- All throughout the day, you are making choices. Sometimes, your choices are conscious and sometimes they're unconscious choices. Nevertheless, they're still choices. The choices you make during every waking moment either add or subtract from your happiness. That's why it's important to practice living more consciously. The more conscious you are, the happier you will be.

Love,
Rebecca

Dear Rebecca,

In your opinion, what's the most important thing a person can do for their well-being?

Signed,

Anonymous

Thank you, Anonymous, for asking such an important question. First of all, let me begin by saying that there are 7.2 billion people on this planet, and each and every one of us has a different perspective and definition of what "well-being" means. I'd love to share with you what well-being means to me, and if you feel my answer resonates with you, yippee!

It was only when I began accepting responsibility for my behavior, my reactions to circumstances, and, ultimately, my attitude toward what was happening "to" me that I began to feel a lasting and unshakable sense of well-being. Honestly, taking responsibility for my well-being is one of the BIGgest challenges I've had in my life. It was so easy-breezy to point the middle finger and blame circumstances and other people for my problems. I'll admit that it took years to really get that I can't control anything or anyone outside of myself. With that said, how could I expect to feel a sense of well-being from anything or anyone outside of myself? I am the only person responsible for the state of my well-being.

I'm at the top of the "well-being" ladder when I know and feel, without a doubt, the following:

- Everything that happens to me happens for my betterment.
- Everything that happens to me is a Universal lesson waiting to be discovered.
- There are no mistakes.
- I'm serving the world by my existence alone. There is nothing I'm supposed to do; only what I am inspired to do.
- Time is an illusion; therefore, I am patient with all things unfolding.
- There is nothing that can stop, slow down, or speed up my Destiny.
- I AM a physical extension of the Universe.
- I AM responsible for my well-being.

Thank you, Anonymous, for the stimulating question.
Love,
Rebecca

Dear Rebecca,

My twenty-something daughter is smart and talented but has an unforgiving and intolerant nature that worries me. She has some OCD tendencies, insomnia, and can't seem to relax. I wonder what I can do, if anything, to help her open up to the wonders of the world and to look for the best in people, rather than the worst, and to be a more kindly, compassionate being? She is far too young to be so cynical, negative, and self-absorbed. Is there anything I can do to guide her, or is this just a passage in her life that I should accept (and love)?

Signed,

What Have I Done?

My dear WHID,

First of all, I want to express my appreciation to you for being open enough to share your challenges with the world. WHID, I can feel your heart; and you, like many mothers, have a natural intention of wanting only what's best for their children. I, too, am a mother, and there was a time in my life when being a "good mother" was my number-one priority. During my well-meaning attempts at being a good mother, I found myself talking—talking a lot. I talked about everything from sex to drugs to money to relationships to religion to politics and everything in between. I expressed what I liked and I expressed what I didn't like. I practically told him how to *be* and what to become.

I shared with him my limited (yes, I said limited) perspectives every chance I got. "Fortunately" for *me*, we lived under the same roof, so he was literally a captive audience.

All joking aside, from the day my son was born, he received the Rebecca L. Norrington doctrine of how to be, act, feel, speak, and think. Oh, I left nothing out. And here's the kicker—I even remember thinking, "If my son turned out to be just like me, I'd be happy." Without question, my good intentions were leading my son down the path to a life of certain unhappiness. Why? Because I was unhappy! I could not teach what I did not possess my own damn self. Ouch! Besides, there couldn't *possibly* be an alternative way of thinking, living, or being other than what *I* thought, could there?

With all of that said, I'd like to provide you with my personal perspective of what's happening with you and your precious daughter. I'm going to dissect every section of your letter down to the least common denominator, to discover what's under the surface of your relationship. I'd like you to know in advance that I'm a hard-hitter—it's just who I am. With that said, my answer is written with an enormous amount of love. My intention is always to (1) find the truth, and then (2) assist you with finding peace.

Your Worrying Has Got to Stop

You wrote that your daughter's behavior "worries me." I believe that worrying is a useless and addictive behavior that was taught to us at an early age. Worry is an emotion that affects the "worrier" detrimentally. Also important to note: the act of worrying subtracts from your happiness. Why would you want to engage in a behavior that is useless *and* subtracts from your happiness? This is a question only you can answer.

Hear Ye, Hear Ye—I'm Worried about You

Further, advertising to anyone that you are worried about them is an interesting behavior to dissect. In my opinion, "I'm worried about you" is an announcement that doesn't need announcing. What does that say about a person who advertises to the object of their concern that they are worried? I used to think that when people told me they were worried about me, it meant that they cared about me. I discovered that is not the truth. What does "I'm worried about you" really mean? In my opinion, one of the reasons you announce that you are worried is because (1) you'd like the person to change their behavior. "Change your behavior so that I don't worry about you," right? Or (2) you might say "I'm worried about you" is another way to express concern for the person. If I worry about you, that means I care about you, right? Wrong. Worrying about someone does not mean you love or care about them. And in my not-so-humble opinion, the opposite is true. The energy of "being worried" brings NOTHING of value to you or the person you're worried about. Nothing! Rebecca, what can I do instead? I'm glad you asked.

I would rather send out to the Universe the following thoughts:

I know and trust that the Universe has total control of what happens to me and my loved ones.

I know and trust that the Universe will not allow anything to happen that's not supposed to happen.

I know and trust that my loved one is experiencing exactly what s/he needs to experience at any given time.

I know and trust that everything that happens to me and my loved ones is happening for my and their betterment.

When you know, trust, and surrender to the perfect order and wisdom of the Universe, what is there to worry about?

The Truth about Worrying

- Worrying is a learned behavior. You were not born with the ability to worry. You were taught to worry. The good news is that whatever you've learned, you can unlearn.

- When you TELL someone you're worried about them, it's really your attempt to control them, in disguise.

- Worrying is an unhealthy addiction.

- When you're worried, you're not living in the present moment. The present moment is REALITY, and the future doesn't exist—yet.

- Worrying serves absolutely no purpose—ever.

Warning: You might need a seatbelt for this next response.

Please know that I'm responding to your question with Universal Love. I'd also like you to know that I'm sharing with you the wisdom of my experience and Universal teachings. My dear mother, you are very judgmental and extremely critical. I know this because I used to be the Queen of Judgment Nation and Ruler of Critical County. It takes one to recognize another one. (Remember that statement.) Yes, you are extremely judgmental and critical; however, I don't believe this behavior begins and ends with your daughter. Usually, people who judge and criticize others also judge and criticize themselves, life, circumstances, events, countries, and the state of the world! It's a miserable party. Judging and criticizing is a manmade behavior. We were not put on this planet to judge or criticize anything or anyone, including ourselves. What I've discovered about my past behavior is that as soon as I stopped judging and criticizing myself, I stopped judging and criticizing others. Why did I decide to end this destructive behavior once and for all? It's really simple: when I judge and criticize, I literally subtract from my happiness. All judgments and critical thoughts subtract from your happiness.

Further, there are millions of people on this planet who would not come to the same conclusions you have regarding your daughter. In fact, if I met your daughter, I guarantee I would not have the same opinion you have about her. Why? Because I'd be experiencing your daughter through *my* eyes. There are 7.2 billion people on this planet, and each person will form a different opinion about your daughter. And this is what I'd tell your daughter: the only opinion that should matter to her is her opinion of herself.

Warning: You WILL need a seatbelt for this response.

This is going to be hard to hear and digest, but all—and I mean all—of the adjectives you used to describe your daughter are really describing YOU, my dear one. Yes, you can only recognize in another what YOU are yourself. It's a truth, which believe me, I resisted for years. Yes, every "fault" I found in someone else was screaming MY name. You cannot notice what's "wrong" with anyone else unless you possess those same characteristics. When you criticize anyone, you're ALWAYS speaking about YOURSELF. Look in the mirror. Do YOU recognize any of the following traits?

- Unforgiving and intolerant nature
- OCD tendencies
- Insomnia
- Can't seem to relax
- Cynical
- Negative
- Self-absorbed

Your letter is not about your daughter. Your letter is about you. You said you wanted to help your daughter, and I believe you really do. The advice you wrote is not for your daughter. The advice you wrote below is for you to follow!

- Open up to the wonders of the world

- Look for the best in people rather than the worst
- Be a kinder, compassionate being

When my son was eleven, I discovered the ONLY way I was going to teach him valuable lessons was for ME to be the example of what I wanted him to learn. Much to my chagrin, my words never taught him anything. It was *my behavior* that influenced him. If you want your daughter to relax, YOU have to be the example of a relaxed person. If you want your daughter to look for the best in people, YOU have to look for the best in people. If you want your daughter to be a more kind and compassionate being, YOU have to be a more kind and compassionate being.

The only thing you can do is BE the example of the type of person you want your daughter to be. BE, LIVE, and REPRESENT the example every day and in every moment. I also suggest that you start focusing on and noticing ONLY the good traits in your daughter. Begin ignoring what you think is "wrong" with her, because in reality, there's nothing wrong with her or her behavior.

In conclusion, my dear mother, know that your daughter has her own journey to walk and experience. She, like you and I, has lessons to learn that are unique to each of us. Allow her to experience her journey in her own way and in her own time. I'd like you to know and trust that the Universe is holding your daughter by the hand along her journey. Everything she does and everything she says and everything that she experiences IS for her betterment. Know that, trust that, and leave your daughter in the hands of the Universe. Mom, the Universe does not make mistakes.

I'm grateful for your questions and I can also feel your loving heart. I would like YOU to know, without a doubt, that I love you and the Universe loves you.

Love,
Rebecca

Hey Rebecca,

Recently, I have been having some trouble with my ego and moving into my heart. What happens is thoughts that are not so constructive constantly enter my head. I am always focusing on the present moment, opening my ears to listen to what's real in the present, putting focus on my heart, and looking at people through the eyes of love and treating them all equal. But these negative thoughts enter my mind over and over, thoughts that judge and keep me in this mind-made world. There seems to be little improvement, and I feel like I have been in the same position for a long time. I've been doing different things like donating to causes that feel right and using the money I have left to give joy to my friends. Every now and then I will get into a state of pure peace and wonder in the present moment, but it just goes back to this mind-made world where I don't feel the power of me moving forward to great things in my life.

Signed,
Randall

Dear Randall,

Thank you for your letter. I love how conscious and self-aware you are. And, Randall, you're already ahead of the game because when you're self-aware and have the ability to live in a conscious state, it's much easier to find solutions to any challenge you experience.

I would also love to live in the present moment 24/7. In my not-so-humble opinion, living in the present moment 24/7 is the ultimate way to live. And the fact that you already know how important living in the moment is to maintaining peace and happiness, lets me know your foundation is directly connected to the Universe. I, too, had issues with my ego's never-ending negative banter before I took *its* power away. Now, for the most part, my ego is a starving entity held in check, when I'm living consciously throughout my day.

The Truth about the Ego

Let's remember: the Universe does not make mistakes, and creating the ego as an entity was necessary to our human evolution. (I think it would be fascinating to know how much we all will evolve in the next 500 years, but I digress.)

I like to think of the ego as a job applicant with a limited amount of skills and functions. YOU have to designate which position you allow your ego to hold. For example: You wouldn't let a five-year-old drive a car. Why? Because the five-year-old isn't qualified to drive. It's the same concept with the ego. In fact, the ego and the five-year-old have some similar traits.

Traits of the Ego
- Needs lots of attention
- Needs to be constantly fed
- Needs to be heard
- Disguises itself as YOU
- Lives in fear of being exposed

Behavior of the Ego
- Bathes in negativity
- Showers in judgments and comparisons
- Dresses in feel-bad activity and feel-bad thoughts
- Lives in fear

Again, the ego possesses a limited amount of skill and function. Problems arise when we allow the ego to hold positions of power that it's not qualified for. My experience with my ego is that it never has anything good to say about me or anyone else. And since I know that, why would I allow that "voice" to make decisions about how I feel about me?

Let me be clear, the ego is not an enemy. The ego has its role, its purpose, and its place. If it weren't for my ego, I'd walk out of the house wearing plaid and paisley prints . . . around my head. I might even refuse to shower or brush my teeth or apply make-up. No, the ego is not the enemy; however, the ego has been allowed to dominate positions that it's not qualified to hold. Allow your ego to be in charge only of the jobs it's qualified for (make-up, hair, and wardrobe), and your life will change.

What We Resist Persists and What We Focus on Grows

Finally, in order for me to find peace with my ego, I had to STOP resisting it. I had to stop the tendency to struggle. I began to accept, allow, and flow with whatever the ego thought. Why not? I recognize the truth when I hear it, and I recognize the opposite of the truth when I hear it. I can't stop the ego from trying its best to make me feel bad, but I can stop resisting its existence, and I can stop giving its words any credence or power. I started by paying less and less attention to the thoughts the ego had and began replacing them with thoughts that served me better.

How I Interact with My Ego

I embrace and accept the ego as an important part of me. I allow the ego to be itself, without judgment and reprimand. Also, I don't resist any thoughts the ego has. Why? Because resisting the ego takes me out of the present moment. Instead of resisting the ego, I just observe and witness. Sometimes, just sometimes, I actually have fun with the ego. When I'm feeling really feisty, I talk back to my ego and say, "Hey, is that all you have for me today?" or "Is that the best you can do to make me feel bad?" When I ask those questions, I usually receive silence in return. Try it.

Change Your Perspective

Change the way you think about your ego. Think of your ego as being a bad reality show on TV. Bad entertainment can be funny. Lighten up. Now that you know the truth about the ego, have some fun and chillax (chill out + relax). Remember, you are not your ego.

Randall also wrote:

"I don't feel the power of me moving forward to great things in my life."

When you say you're dissatisfied because you don't feel the power of moving forward to "great things in my life," know that that thought is spoken by none other than Mr. Ego. Remember, your ego has one job and one job only—to keep you in a state of dissatisfaction, for as long as possible. That's why it's so important to know the difference between the two "voices." The truth is that the Universe would tell you, "Randall, your life is unfolding in the exact manner it's supposed to unfold." Further, the Universe would tell you to relax and start appreciating and loving where you are NOW. Life evolves and changes. Randall, your life is also evolving and changing in every moment. Know that. Trust that. The Universe knows what IT is doing. By the way, you'll continue to experience great things, and even more great things; however, the Universe wants you to love and embrace were you are now: the present moment. Surrender to the plan of the Universe and relax. Your life is unfolding in perfect order. You might want to re-read The Bitter Pill of Dissatisfaction.

Randall additionally wrote:

Also, when I am at social gatherings, I find it hard to get into a conversation with people. Like, no words will come to my mind. I just smile and try to be at peace with myself, but I see everybody in a conversation except me. Then on certain occasions, I will get into a conversation where it feels like everything is going perfect and the way it should. It just feels like a lot of confusion at this point in my life.

My dear Randall,

The first thing I would say to you is STOP trying so hard. I've found that when I struggle with anything, it's because I'm disconnected from the Universe. Have you ever seen a rose bush struggle to bloom? Have you seen a dog struggle to be a dog? Have you ever witnessed the sun struggle to shine? Whenever I'm struggling, I know the Universe is NOT involved. Further, it's not the event that's causing your struggle. It's your thoughts about the event that are causing your struggle.

Who Am I?

One of the hardest things I've had to learn was to just be myself. The reason why it was so hard to be me is because I didn't even know who I was! I spent years discarding layers and layers of someone else's stuff. It was like I had someone else living in my body. Now that I'm learning who I am, I know what feels like a fit and I know what feels like a shoe that's three sizes too small. Yes, it's taken me decades to be at peace with who I really am. Who am I? I'm happy, fun, funny, light, introvert, extrovert, and a hippie who expresses herself trough teaching fitness classes, speaking, and writing. When

I attend social gatherings, I don't know how I'm going to feel when I arrive. Sometimes I'm quiet and observe other people and sometimes I feel like chatting. Either way, I'm okay with whatever I feel inspired to be and do in the moment.

Let me share a real-life experience that I recently had at a social gathering: my high school reunion. While in high school, I was shy and socially awkward with a total of two friends. Yes, I said two friends. And to make it worse, I didn't even like them. I was hanging out with them because I thought it was odd for me to be alone. I thought it was weird not to have friends.

When I attended my reunion, I was basically the same type of social person (introvert and extrovert), with one major difference: I was very comfortable being me. I was happy in my skin. Because I wasn't one of the "popular kids" and I wasn't a member of a "clique," I remember thinking before I arrived that I was going to be okay if I talked to anyone and I was going to be okay if I didn't talk to anyone. And, it was also going to be okay if no one talked to me! I was ready.

When I arrived, I purposely decided to sit at a table far from the "action." I did what I was inspired to do in the moment, which was to observe other people enjoying the evening. My entertainment came in the form of *people-watching*. The only people I talked to that evening were people sitting at my table or fellow classmates who made the long trek across the room to speak to me.

Quiet as a Mouse

There were ten people sitting at my table. Half of the people sitting at my table were husbands or wives of my classmates. A gentleman sitting to my left was the husband of a classmate. This man didn't utter one word to any one of us at the table the entire evening. In fact, he spoke only to his wife when she engaged him in conversation. When his wife left the table to socialize, he sat quietly in silence. Even though he didn't speak to anyone at the table, there was a peace about him that I definitely felt. He was very comfortable not speaking. You, my dear Randall, are not. Why? It's a question that only you will discover the answer to. If you ask me, and you did, there's nothing wrong with attending a social gathering and not uttering a word, if you are at peace with yourself.

Love,
Rebecca

Dear Rebecca,

I'm totally overwhelmed by the state of my life. We had a huge financial setback ($500K) because of a poorly thought-out investment that my husband wanted and then held onto for way too long, despite all the signs and my urging. So, now we need to reevaluate and rebuild. Moreover, since I was rear-ended in January, I've been in physical therapy, etc., and on the mend. I'm slow to get around and tire easily. I'm trying to put the pieces back together, for the most part alone, and it is sucking up all my time. My spouse has moved on to his next pet project, has not been very approachable, and takes on almost no responsibility. He is fairly clueless and believes that my workload should be manageable, and that I just take on too many personal projects. I've been trying to talk to him for years but he is not approachable.

This is not the life I had envisioned. Once upon a time, I faced each day with excitement, filled with creative ideas. Nowadays, I wake up each day and almost dread the relentless amount of work before me. From the time I open my eyes until the time I crawl to bed. I am working on resolving my children's health issues and also home-school my teenage son, who has a disability. Sometimes I feel like I have to be both mother and father to my son to give him the guidance he needs, since my spouse acts more like a babysitter than a loving parent. I'm feeling less and less like there is much hope that things will improve, even though there is much in my life to be grateful for. A sense of gratitude does help keep me going day to day. What else am I missing here? How can I make this marriage work? What steps do I need to take to find deeper happiness and satisfaction?

Signed,

Questions

Dear Questions,

Your letter is filled with a lot of personal questions and life challenges that daily subtract from your happiness. Believe me when I say that I can understand your feelings of being overwhelmed with life. You listed several circumstances and issues that I will address one by one. As always, my intention is to (1) find the truth, and then (2) assist you with finding peace.

One of the most obvious themes in your letter is your focus on what's wrong with your life instead of focusing on what's right with your life. I read and re-read what you wrote. Your letter is laced with criticism, dissatisfaction, frustration, gloom, misery, sadness, and unhappiness. I'm not using those words to be mean and or unsympathetic. I'm using those descriptive words to make a point. There isn't one person, including myself, who hasn't felt like you are feeling at more than one time in our lives. You are not alone. Life is filled with up and downs, challenges, and bumpy roads. You cannot escape what life brings. You cannot control what life unfolds. You cannot escape the journey. What you can do is change your perspective about your reality. Your perspectives have to change for your life to change.

360 Choices to Happiness

There are 360 degrees in a complete circle. There is no beginning or ending to a circle. And there is no beginning or ending to Energy. You are Energy. You are conscious Energy. Because you are conscious Energy you have the ability to choose what to focus on. This is a mandatory concept to understand if you want to be happy. At any given moment, we have 360 different ways to respond and or label any circumstance we experience. Let me be clear: it's not easy to choose another perspective, but it is possible to shift your focus with (1) intention and (2) practice.

Intention and Commitment

You must have the intention and the commitment to focus on what's good in your life during every moment. You can verbalize your intention as soon as you wake up. It's simple and easy. All you need to do is say out loud, before you get out of bed, "My intention for this day is to focus on what's good in my life." In fact, you can practice saying that as many times as you want during the day. In the beginning this practice might not seem to be effective and you probably will continue to focus on what's wrong for awhile; however, as with any new skill, you will get better and better at changing your focus. Know that when you make an intention, the Universe always listens.

I also want to say that whatever is happening in your life is supposed to be happening for a reason that you might not be able to comprehend right now. Yes, everything happens for a reason. When I'm challenged by life, I know without a doubt that the challenge is needed and the challenge is here for me to elevate to a higher level of growth and understanding. All challenges are good—regardless of how they might make you feel. All challenges bring an opportunity for personal and spiritual growth. All challenges bring an opportunity for you to shine brighter.

You mentioned you have children. How do you want your children to face challenges? Do you want your children to focus on what's wrong with their lives? Or do you want your children to find peace and happiness with whatever life brings them? Do you want your children to be able to meet every challenge life brings them with gratitude and acceptance? Your children are watching you, and more importantly, your children are feeling your energy. Be the living example of how to navigate through life!

Your Husband and Making Marriage Work

Your words are screaming a limited perspective.

"My spouse has moved on to his next pet project, has not been very approachable, and takes on almost no responsibility. He is fairly clueless..."

"I've been trying to talk to him for years, but he is not approachable..."

"My spouse acts more like a babysitter than a loving parent."

"How can I make this marriage work?"

My dear Questions, how do you expect to "make this marriage work" when you harbor feelings of resentment and disdain for your husband? It sounds like (at least in this letter) that you share none of the responsibility for the state of your marriage. To begin with, you are extremely critical of your husband. It's interesting because there was a time in my life where I too was extremely critical of my ex-husband, along with being critical of everybody else I knew. Criticizing others was a daily habit of mine. First, there is one huge problem with criticizing anyone and that is you subtract from your happiness when you do that. Second, when you criticize anyone, the words you use are actually meant for you to hear. Ouch! So ask yourself the following:

- Am I ever non-approachable? When does this happen, and why?
- Are there times or specific occasions when I take on almost no responsibility? When does this happen, and why?
- Are there times when I am or act fairly clueless? When does this happen, and why?
- Are there times when I act more like a babysitter than a loving parent? When does this happen, and why?
- Are there times when I act more like a babysitter than a loving partner? When does this happen, and why?

Now, when are YOU going to change?

Gratitude

There are 7.2 billion people on this planet, and I'm sure that more than one person would love to trade places with you. Why? You have a home. You have food. You have children. You physically survived a car accident with the ability to walk again. (I have a dear friend who has been paralyzed since high school). You have a husband who is his own person. I could go on, but I'm sure you get my point.

Another Perspective

Let me share two real-life stories. I have a girlfriend who at thirty-six years old attracted breast cancer. Her reaction? According to her own words, contracting cancer was a "gift from God to her and her family." Why? Because before the cancer, she took her own existence for granted. She let small things bother her. She was easy to anger. She found fault with her life and her family. She was living without feelings of gratitude and appreciation for life itself. Her diagnosis changed her life. Her diagnosis changed her perspective. She chose to view her diagnosis as a gift.

I met a blind man on the bus last year. I purposely sat next to him and asked him how he had become blind. He told me he was hit on the back of the head with a baseball bat and lost his sight. He was twenty-one at the time. He then went on to tell me that he was grateful for losing his sight! He told me being blind saved his life! He told me being blind was a gift from God. How could this be possible, I asked? His story was not unique. As a young man, he was a member of a street gang. His daily "to-do" list consisted of gangbanging, stealing, and murder. He even admitted to participating in dismembering and disposing of bodies. The blind man told me he would have surely been in prison or dead, if he hadn't stopped his behavior. The baseball bat to the back of his head saved his life, and more importantly, he was grateful and appreciative. Now he shares his story with young men who are in gangs or at risk of following in his footsteps.

You commented that your husband says you take on too many personal projects? Is this true? What are they? Do they conflict with the time you need to focus on your priorities? What are your priorities? What can YOU do to create a livable, sustainable balance between your priorities and your personal projects? I support you and understand that we all need something that's just for us, especially when we give of ourselves to others on a daily basis. Please continue to engage in whatever nourishes your soul.

Lastly, you wrote, "This is not the life I had envisioned." Life is never about what we envision, my dear Questions. Life is what the Universe envisions for us. After decades of suffering due to resisting reality, I've finally surrendered and realized that I do not have control over what happens to me. Because if I did, I would have designed my life a whole lot differently than how it has unfolded. What I do have control over is my perspective, my attitude, my focus, my intentions, my words, my beliefs, and my behavior. Finally, I trust and surrender to whatever the Universe has in store for me. The

Universe knows what each of us needs to experience. Know this and trust it.

Do you want to be happy and at peace? Let go, be grateful for your life, and start living.

Love,
Rebecca

Dear Rebecca,

What are some suggestions you would make to someone who is talented but just can't see how good they really are?

Signed,
BC

Dear BC,

I usually don't answer third-party questions about *other* people. With that said, *know* that the person you are speaking of is on his or her own path of journey and discovery. By the way, one of the ways *you* subtract from *your* happiness is noticing what other people are doing.

Love,
Rebecca

RealitySpirituality: The Truth About Happiness

Dear Rebecca,

When a person is run by ego, based on the books I've read, it is actually self-destructive. It's important not to confuse ego with self-confidence and self-esteem—a person should not feel badly about themselves; however, ego puts your thinking outside of the present and actually can cause depression and bad feelings. Thoughts?

Signed,

BC

Dear BC,

You don't have a question, and your statements are generic in nature. I would love to be of assistance; however, it's difficult for me to grasp what you need. Please write in again and ask me something specific that YOU need guidance with, and I will be happy to help.

Love,

Rebecca

Dear Rebecca,

I don't like to admit this, but I am unhappy with other people's success. It doesn't even matter if I know the person or not. I always notice what someone else has that I don't have. I have struggled with this for years and have not found an answer that will rid me of this awful behavior. It's not that

I don't want them to have their success, but I feel I deserve success too. Can you please help me with this?

Signed,

Envious

My dear Envious,

I love, love, love your question. Believe me when I tell you that you are not alone with this dilemma. Don't tell anyone, but I was guilty of the same type of behavior . . . for years. It was really hard for me to fake enjoyment if I thought I deserved the same things I was coveting. And as you said, I did not want to deny anyone else their good fortune, but I always wondered when my *pot of gold* was going to arrive at my door. I was stuck for quite a while, until I asked the Universe for help. As you know, when you ask it is always given.

I asked, "Universe, why am I bothered when someone else experiences what I want to experience? Why can't I be happy for someone else's good fortune?" I should have asked a lot sooner and saved myself years of misery because the answer came very quickly. The reality is *I* am not bothered! My ego is the one that's bothered! I AM NOT my ego. I am a physical extension of the Universe and, therefore, I truly am not bothered. I AM NOT dissatisfied with someone else's success, but my ego sure was dissatisfied.

It was time for me to finally realize, accept, and remember that there are two separate entities/energies living inside of me. One is the ego and the other one is the Universe. How I feel depends solely on which entity/energy I pay attention to!

Love,

Rebecca

Dear Rebecca,

I thought a marriage is about give and take and mutual support. I keep giving, but now I am resentful because it's not mutual. My husband is good at taking and thinks mostly of himself. His actions are guided by doing what makes him happy. He shies away from responsibility. But he follows your principles of making self happy, putting his own happiness above all else. Example: When my son was fourteen years old and doing poorly in school, and clinically depressed, my husband was busy making plans to travel to New York to teach a workshop. That's the part about the pursuit of self-happiness that I don't quite understand. And I get it: I have to look out for myself and create my own happiness. I'm married to someone who is looking out for himself. I'm not faulting him, but it's taken me twenty years and a major financial set-back to recognize the imbalance and why I feel so drained.

Dear Drained,

I am going to respond to you without a single reference to your husband. What your husband did, does, or doesn't do has nothing to do with you or your happiness. Furthermore, your circumstances, including your child's health, have nothing to do with your happiness. Nothing.

Let me be perfectly clear. It's not your fault for thinking other people and various circumstances are responsible for your happiness. That's what we all are taught at a very early age: Someone else is responsible for our happiness; something else is responsible for our happiness. Take a look at the media. There's always someone else to blame. I did it. I placed the blame on everyone except myself as to why I was so unhappy. My dear Drained, the reason you feel discontentment and unhappiness is coming from inside of you. And contrary to what you think, the reason **why** you feel "so drained" is because your focus has been on everything and everyone else other than you.

The formula for happiness never includes another equation other than you. Everyone else is excluded including children, spouses, parents, friends, co-workers, cashiers, bus drivers, medical staff, travel agents, astronauts, animals, and the mailman. This is a very powerful concept to "get" because now you—and you alone—are solely responsible for your happiness. Let me repeat. **You are responsible for your happiness.** Spiderman, who quoted Voltaire, said, "With great power comes great responsibility."

Now that you know the truth, what are you going to do about it? As I see it, you only have two choices: (1) You can power-up and take on the responsibility for your happiness or (2) you can continue to feel powerless and make excuses and blame other people and or circumstances for your unhappiness. I look at life like this: If I'm solely responsible for my happiness, and I am, what do I need to do now? What do I need to change? How do I change? How do I integrate this new information into my daily life? I'm glad you asked. Here's how.

You want to be happy? Practice the following every day, for the rest of your life.

- STOP criticizing (yourself or others)
- STOP complaining (about yourself or others)
- STOP judging (yourself or others)
- STOP expecting anything from anyone
- STOP blaming someone else for your unhappiness
- STOP having opinions about what someone else is doing
- STOP discussing anyone else unless its complimentary (including yourself)
- STOP focusing on what's wrong

Now you don't have to practice any of the above. But I promise you that if you don't, you will remain unhappy. You want to be happy? "Unlearn" what you've learned and

- START accepting people just as they are
- START allowing people to be themselves, without judgment
- START taking deeper breaths throughout your day
- START focusing on what's good in your Life
- START becoming more self-aware

- START being honest with yourself
- START living consciously
- START making small changes
- START looking in the mirror for answers
- START asking the Universe for guidance

Remember, every time you criticize, complain, judge, blame, have expectations, and focus on "what's wrong," you literally subtract from *your* happiness. Now that you know the truth, what are **YOU** going to do about it? Remember, your happiness is never, and I repeat, never dependent on anyone else. I don't care what they're doing or what they are not doing. No one has the power to make you unhappy.

Finally, I'd like you to know that you will find the happiness you seek if you are willing to journey on the road less traveled. The reason why people are not as happy as they could be is because they are **not willing to commit** to the arduous daily task of monitoring all moments. It's called living consciously and becoming self-aware.

Warning: **Taking responsibility for your OWN happiness is not necessarily easy, pleasant, or fun.**

University of Happiness Attendance Guidelines

You're in training every day, including weekends. You don't take vacations. You're always on duty without lunch or breaks. And you're constantly looking in the mirror because that's where all your answers are. The only time-off you get is when you're sleeping. When you're ready to make that type of moment-by-moment commitment, I promise you, you will live happily ever after. Heaven *is* on Earth, patiently waiting for you to discover it.

P.S. I want you to know how much I love your courage to share the truth of your experience with the world. Every single one of us is not without multiple challenges. You are exceptional because you're asking the tough questions. You're asking tough questions because you want answers. Why do you want answers? Because you want to be happy.

A short time later, rln writes:

Dear Drained,

I want you to know that this is your time. It's time to make changes and begin living happily ever after. I have an important question for you. If I asked your husband about the marriage, what would he say? There are always two sides to every story. I'm curious: Are you able to create a list as to what your husband would say about you? Be honest. Honesty brings freedom and clarity. Think about that and write back.

Love,
Rebecca

Drained writes back:

He would say that:
- We have a lot of issues that need to be worked out, and it will take time
- I repeat myself
- I don't listen
- It's not tit for tat (I want "compensation" for what I do)
- I compare our marriage to other marriages
- We have a long history
- I am "all over the place" with discussions, I am hard to talk to, and impossible to have a meaningful discussion with
- I am too pointed in my comments
- I start too many projects
- I don't put things away
- I am disorganized and I should do things the way he suggested.

I've written down all the things I do (taxes, monthly bills, managing property, remodeling rental property, homeschooling, grocery shopping, cooking, tending to kid's health issues, financial planning, gardening, etc.). And I asked him to mark those that he feels are most important. All other things will either be hired out or given less priority. This was about two or three years ago, and he claims he responded and returned the sheet of paper. Then he said maybe he still has it because

I certainly did not get it. (I wrote it down because he was generally too "busy" when I asked to have a talk in person).

The only responsibilities he has (meaning things he can be relied upon to do on a regularly basis) is he brings in the mail. He does other things, but if he has the time, and does not want it to be responsible. He doesn't acknowledge that I do just about everything in the house. If he doesn't acknowledge it, then he doesn't have to give credit. Somewhere along the line, that's where I started to get resentful and lost the joy.

Here's my second enlightened moment. I've been taking on more and more each year. The more I did, he'd be happy, but only for a while. Then I'd have to do more and more until we are here and I do just about everything in the house. Maybe I thought it would help him by taking care of business. Maybe if he was happy, then our marriage would be better. Or, that he would love me more. And, sometimes it was easier to just do it than wait for him to get around to it and/or avoid a big discussion. In all fairness, I definitely have my flaws and my own neuroses and am not easy to live with. I am trying to recall all his other complaints. He has a lot, for sure. That's about all I can recall for now.

Rebecca responds:

Please remember that when I answer you, it's always my intention to (1) find the truth and (2) assist you with finding peace.

This might be difficult to hear but the truth is that if your husband did everything you asked him to and he behaved exactly the way you wanted him to, you would still be unhappy. Why? Because happiness is an inside job—period. One of the reasons for your frustration is you think that if your husband changed, you'd be happy. I'm here to tell you, unequivocally, that is not the case. Your husband is not the source of your unhappiness.

Remember:

- Your happiness does not depend on what anyone else says.
- Your happiness does not depend on what anyone else doesn't say.
- Your happiness does not depend on what anyone does.
- Your happiness does not depend on what anyone else doesn't do.
- Your happiness does not depend on your circumstances either, regardless of what they are.

Unless you engage in a daily moment-by-moment commitment to growing beyond who you are now, you will never find the happiness you seek. Happiness comes from within. There are no exceptions. The road to happiness begins and ends with the person in the mirror.

What Else Is Wrong?

A second issue, according to you, is that you carry the majority of the household responsibility. Let's say that's true.

Let me share with you what I've learned about "giving of myself" and happiness. Whenever I decide to give someone something, whether it's my time, or an actual gift, or take on added responsibilities like the example you stated earlier, I make the decision and choice to give without expecting anything back in return—including expecting a thank-you. In other words, I give without strings or conditions attached.

I didn't always have that perspective—give without expectations of anything in return. In fact, the majority of my life I unconsciously and sometimes consciously gave to get something back in return. What were some of the things I wanted in return? What I wanted varied from love, time, attention, kindness, praise, acknowledgement, credit, compassion, concern, sympathy, friendship, responsiveness, and money, to name a few examples of what I *expected* when I extended myself just as you stated earlier.

Happiness Is Always My Priority

While on my journey of prioritizing happiness, I learned that when I give I cannot expect anything in return. I have to give without strings or conditions attached to whatever I'm giving. As I mentioned before, I can't even expect a thank-you. Why? Because expectations subtract from happiness. Expectations always subtract from happiness. My dear Drained, you have so many expectations, it's no wonder you are so unhappy.

A Few Characteristics of Happy People

- Happy people don't expect anything from anyone.
- Happy people don't complain.
- Happy people don't compare themselves to others.
- Happy people don't get angry too often, and if they do, they realize their anger has nothing to do with another person or an existing circumstance.
- Happy people don't try to control anyone else.
- Happy people don't talk negatively about others or themselves.
- Happy people are conscious and aware of the energy they emit.
- Happy people take responsibility for their own happiness.
- Happy people know they cannot change anyone but themselves.
- Happy people are kind.
- Happy people are patient.
- Happy people accept others unconditionally.
- Happy people are not critical.
- Happy people don't make judgments.
- Happy people are self-aware.
- Happy people don't blame others for their unhappiness.
- Happy people do not create drama.
- Happy people live in the moment.
- Happy people don't try to change anyone else.
- Happy people are constantly evolving into happier people.
- Happy people spread happiness.

- Happy people know that their happiness depends on the person in the mirror.

Now, the only reason I can vouch for all of the above is because I used to be extremely unhappy and the opposite of everything I listed above. I was one of the most miserable persons you'd ever want to meet. I was trapped in a cycle of blaming and finger-pointing. I was easily offended, easily irritated, quick to anger, bossy, opinionated, controlling, confrontational, moody, critical, and I needed to be right—about everything. Need I go on? Did I want to be happy? Had you asked me that question then, I would have said, "Of course I do." However, I had no clue that my behavior was literally sucking and subtracting the happiness out of my life. When I discovered that my former behavior and my need to be happy weren't compatible, I was forced to change my behavior. And, I don't mind admitting any of the above, because, quite frankly, I'm very proud of the behaviors I chose to eliminate from my life.

Finally

So, you see, it's up to you, and only you, to make all the necessary changes if you want to be happy. It's up to you to change your perspectives. It's up to you to change your behavior. It's up to you to choose your focus. It's up to you to become a happy person.

I guarantee that when you change, your life changes. You have the power and ability to be happy, regardless of your circumstances and regardless of what anyone else does, says, or doesn't say or do. Now that you know the truth about happiness, the ball is in your court. You can change your life, but you have to change you first.

Warning: Finding peace and happiness is found on the road less traveled. And that road is less traveled for a reason. Your journey is going to be never-ending, extremely difficult, and brutally challenging. However the reward is heaven on Earth.

Love,
Rebecca

RealitySpirituality Radio Show—January 2014

A woman called in searching for answers.

Caller: I'm feeling disillusioned by what is happening in my life. I'm waiting for a decision, and I don't think it will turn out well.

Rebecca: If you look back in your life, have you ever noticed that everything that has happened to you was for a good reason?

Caller: No. I cannot say that. People are taking things away from me.

RealitySpirituality: The Truth About Happiness

Rebecca: What do you mean? External things?

Caller: Yes. My career. People are sabotaging me.

Rebecca: There are 360 different ways to look at the same circumstance, in order to find happiness and peace. Is there any way you can change your perspective and find something good in what is happening to you now?

Caller: No. You can't help me, can you? Why don't you just say that you don't have any answers?

Rebecca: I answered you.

Click. She hung up.

———

When I was in my twenties, the Universe spoke to me but I was not able to hear that Voice.
When I was in my thirties, the Universe spoke to me but I was not able to hear that Voice.
When I was in my forties, the Universe spoke to me and I began to hear that Voice.
Now it's the only Voice I hear. ~rln

———

RealitySpirituality Radio Show—February 15, 2014

A woman called in to my radio show this morning. Her name was Tina. She asked if I do physic readings, and I told her no. She sounded disappointed but I still asked her why she called? She told me she wanted to know what was going to *happen* between her and *Louis*. She said she wanted to get married, and said they'd shared a wonderful day together on Valentine's Day (2014). She wanted to know if he was going to marry her. I asked how long they had been seeing each other. She paused for a long time then said, "Quite awhile." I asked her how long? "A long time," she replied. I pressed on. Five years? Ten? Fifteen? "What's a long time?" I asked. Tina was silent and refused to respond to the question. The exact reason why she didn't want to tell me how long she had been dating Louis could have been a myriad of reasons. Maybe she thought I would judge her? Maybe she was embarrassed or ashamed to admit how long it had been? Maybe she's a private person? Only Tina knows the answer. One thing I do know is that if you cannot admit how long you've been dating a person, there is a reason why.

When I felt Tina's energy, I was inspired to tell her that even though I'm not a physic, I was going to make a *prediction*. I told her, "Whatever is happening between you and Louis today is going to happen tomorrow. Whatever you are experiencing today, you will experience it again tomorrow. Nothing is going to change unless you change."

With that said, Tina hung up.

Note: When you are able to tell yourself the truth, you are free. When you are not able to tell yourself the truth, you will live in bondage. Some people live their entire lives in bondage. No judgment here, I'm merely stating a fact.

A Facebook Friend responded to this Facebook post of mine: *The best response to an insult is to not respond at all.*

FB Friend: Very difficult strategy to adhere to. Also, if you don't respond, wouldn't the insulting person just think they are right?

Rebecca: What a great question. Let me ask you this. Who's more powerful: The person who can ignore a comment without "retribution" or the person who responds? The way we grow is always a "difficult strategy to adhere to." Growth is difficult. That's why too few people make a commitment to personal growth.

Further, responding is a learned behavior. All behavior that is learned can be unlearned. Think about it. If you insulted a two-year-old, the two-year-old would not "feel" the insult. The toddler hasn't yet learned that insults have (imagined) power. In fact, you could call a baby all kinds of names and the baby would just look at you and accept all of your words without feeling insulted.

The only reason—and I repeat—the only reason anyone is offended or insulted is because they BELIEVE whatever is being said about them.

Your ego is the entity that feels the need to respond... not your Spiritual Self. When you allow your ego to "drive," get ready to crash head first into a brick wall.

"If you don't respond, wouldn't the insulting person just think they are right?" It doesn't matter what anyone else thinks about you. It only matters what you and the Universe think about you.

Thank you for the stimulating comment.

Remember the nursery rhyme: "Copycat, copycat, sitting on the fence, trying to make a dollar out of fifteen cents?" Someone asked me, "How do I make a dollar out of fifteen cents?" Answer: Place fifteen cents in a large bowl. Add trust in the Universe, and mix both ingredients together. Keep trusting and keep mixing, and soon you will have a dollar.

CHAPTER 14

REBECCA L. NORRINGTON QUOTES

CHOICES

Death is inevitable; how you respond to death is a choice. You can't be angry and grateful at the same time. Which one are you going to choose?

If you are unhappy, you can change your perspective in an instant.

If you spend time improving yourself, you will not have time to criticize others.

The only way you can treat someone like they're important is if *you* feel important.

You choose your attitude.

The Universe is expressing Its Self through you. Be mindful of your expression.

When I am faced with any situation that requires me to make a choice, I know which behaviors are aligned with the Universe and which behaviors are not. Yes, after decades of suffering, it has become easy for me to distinguish between

Universal behaviors and manmade behaviors. I am tuned into a Universal Voice that is always present and always provides answers.

I felt a vibrational shift today: I found myself annoyed by the smallest things. That's my sign to take a couple days off to hibernate.

Before you start your day, choose a focus. Example: today, focus on finding good in every person, in every moment, and in every experience.

Look in the mirror and ask yourself this question: what are your priorities? Your priorities determine how you live your life.

Nothing stays the same. We are all evolving into whatever we focus on. Choose your focus. Choose your journey.

WISDOM

I contend that unless you're creating or learning something new, you really aren't thinking at all. Thinking requires thoughts and actions that have never existed before. Thinking requires creativity. A new invention. A composed piece of music. Writing a book, and so on. Anyone that is actively engaged in active learning or creating is thinking. Anything else is simply recycling. Recycling thoughts is not thinking.

Remember, we all are as different as our fingerprints, and our relationship with the Universe is just as unique and personal.

Heaven is a state of mind.
Freedom is a state of mind.

RealitySpirituality: The Truth About Happiness

Heaven is a thought away.

Trust your intuition ... always.

God experiences life *through* you.

The road less traveled is my favorite path.

If you don't know who you are, don't rest ... until you do.

Focus on the good in all that you experience, and you will find it.

You cannot keep secrets and be free at the same time.

You are a physical extension of the Universe.

Your journey and your lessons are uniquely your own.

When you know you are eternal, you will develop patience.

When you know everything is in order, you will develop trust.

When you know everything that happens to you has an ultimate purpose for your betterment, you will develop wisdom.

When you know there is nothing you *have* to do, you will find peace.

When you know who you *really* are, you will always be happy.

It's a tragedy to know the price of everything and the value of nothing.

Life is easy—when you surrender to the Universe's plan.

"Happily ever after" is possible, when you're committed to finding it.

The ego is the "best" recycler: it recycles and relives the same old, sad, angry, unhappy stories for years.

Everything that happens to you is in Devine Order.

Everything that happens to you is for your betterment.

We are here to discover who we are. We are here to be joyful.

Live in the world, free of the world.

When you allow the ego to be in charge, get ready to feel bad.

When you compare yourself to anyone, you subtract from your happiness.

The cause of unhappiness has nothing to do with what happens to you. The cause of your unhappiness is how you perceive what's happened to you.

Our experiences are endless, while our choices are not.

It's time to take a deep breath and relax. Your life is perfect!

Spiritual reality is beyond the intellect.

The Universe is patiently waiting for each of us to discover our Selves. The discovery is inevitable and without a scheduled completion date.

Peace is finding meaning in disorder.

You teach others by your example instead of your words.

Your reaction or response to everything determines what you are going to experience.

What you send out, you will receive.

Relax. Nothing is that serious, especially when you know that you *are* eternal, immortal, universal, and infinite.

The thrill of soaring comes with the fear of falling. Trust that the Universe will NEVER let you fall.

If you've learned something, you can also unlearn it if it no longer serves you.

When you look at Others, you are really looking at Self.

"Know thyself" is easier said than done.

Everything you need is found within—there are no exceptions.

Whatever you think you need from another, you already have it within.

When you change, the world changes.

Stay out of everyone else's business because they're on their own path.

Eliminate the word "should" from your vocabulary and you will be happier.

Change how you view your life, and you will change your life.

You can't slow it down and you can't speed it up. The truth is that if the Universe wants you to experience "it," you cannot stop "it" from happening. And if the Universe does not want you to experience "it," you cannot make "it" happen. Don't you think it's time to breathe, relax, flow, and enjoy the ride?

You are a physical extension of the Universe.

Human suffering is completely unnecessary when you surrender to the Universe.

I've learned that what I used to think, which kept me unhappy, doesn't work anymore.

Whatever you're thinking and or doing today might change tomorrow. And that's okay.

The only commitment I'm willing to make is my commitment to my spiritual growth.

Changing your mind is okay.

There is no beginning or ending to creation. We are all a part of what is created. We are created with the same *stuff* that creates universes, galaxies, planets, stars, and moons. We are a physical extension of the Universe.

Whenever you resist reality, you become unbalanced. When you struggle with reality, you actually struggle with the same entity that creates worlds. Struggling against the order of the Universe makes no sense. It never feels good to struggle. You never win. You never feel good. You will never be at peace.

The world loves and accepts me just as I am.

I am everything, and everything is within me.

Choose your labels wisely.

Do you want to know what power is? Finding balance in a rocky boat.

You are the answer to all of your "problems."

You can make any sound you hear into music.

If you have ninety-nine "problems," that means that you have ninety-nine opportunities to grow. Have fun outgrowing your problems!

Would you like to lighten your load? Let the Universe decide when, where, what, and how.

Ask the Universe questions and stay open for all possible answers.

Who are you? When you know the answer to that question, you will discover heaven on Earth.

I've eliminated the word "should" from my vocabulary. There is nothing I should do. There is only what I am inspired to do.

You are not meant to struggle. When you struggle, you're actually pushing against the Universe. Stop struggling (which is the same as resisting) and start flowing with it ALL.

Begin each day with gratitude and appreciation for the moments ahead, and you will experience even more miracles.

Is there a difference between our internal and external world? Some say no. I say YES. It's just like football. There is an offense and a defense team. Neither is on the field at the same time, because they have two separate functions. Two separate functions, ONE Team.

Surrender to it all. Surrender with no expectations of "receiving" anything in return. Because when you surrender, you *are* receiving.

Even when things are seemingly going "wrong," they're still right.

What are your priorities? Your priorities will determine your life's journey.

Problems are opportunities to grow in disguise.

What's important to you may not be important to someone else. And that's okay. It doesn't mean they're against you. It just means they are different.

When you remain open to all possibilities, you will discover miracles in every moment.

What if you celebrated each day as though it was your last? Can you imagine how much you would invest in each moment?

LOVE

Unconditional Love defined: I love you regardless of what you do and regardless of what you don't do.

Universal Love is unconditional.

You cannot attach conditions and or strings to Love.

Love is not possessive. True Love wants you to be free.

True love has no strings attached.

When you are patient with someone (including yourself), it's just another way to express love. You cannot love without patience being present.

I love what you are now and I love what you are becoming.

Looking for someone to fall in love with? How about looking in the mirror? The greatest love of all is with Self.

TRUTH

It's impossible to be angry *with* someone. The truth is that your anger is a reflection of what's really going on inside of you. Your emotions always reflect your internal state.

Do you know what's missing in the animal kingdom? Judgments, blame, labels, comparing, expectations, et cetera.

Animals live in the present moment. That's why they are at peace with the world.

If you *have* to be right, then something's wrong.

The Truth does not hurt. The Truth sets you free.

Suffering occurs when you label any situation as bad. Change the label; and your suffering ends immediately.

If you're offended, it means you believe what's being said. You cannot be offended unless you believe the offense.

Life's journey starts from within and stays within. Everything you need in this life is within.

There is no requirement to tell the truth to others, but we are required to tell the truth to ourselves.

You are not the stories in your head—you are much more.

Who are you without your titles and accomplishments? You are a child of the Universe.

No event or life experience has a meaning until YOU give it a meaning.

Words are as powerful as you allow them to be.

You have to be willing to be uncomfortable in order to grow.

Embrace uncertainty, and you will live aligned with the Universe.

You don't have to wait to experience heaven. Heaven is a state of mind. Heaven is this moment. Heaven is on Earth.

Just because you're in a conversation with someone doesn't mean they are interested in what you have to say.

Do you have to agree with someone to have a peaceful relationship? I say no. What you do have to do is accept their perspectives without judgment. Only then will the relationship flow peacefully.

When you allow words to have power over you, you lose your power.

Are you able to accept everyone without judgment? When you do, you align with the Universe. The Universe does not judge. The sun shines on us all.

Can you blame anyone else for how you feel? *Shhhhh . . .* don't tell anyone, but I used to. Until I realized that how I feel is my responsibility.

All negative thoughts are thoughts that are untrue. The Universe does not label anything negative. All negative thoughts are manmade.

The truth is: it's all an illusion, anyway.

PATIENCE

Time is a manmade illusion. You can never waste what you have an abundance of.

It took 4.5 billion years for the Universe to create our Earth. I want the patience of the Universe.

Trust that the Universe has impeccable timing.

When you have patience with others, you are expressing love for them.

HAPPINESS

Your thoughts about your circumstances determine whether or not you are happy. Change your thoughts, change your life.

A handicap is the inability to be happy.

In my opinion, the only successful people are happy people.

Surrender; accept what is . . . and you will live happily ever after.

At any given moment, people are as happy as they decide to be. Happiness is a choice.

When you have an agenda, you will also have expectations. Agendas and expectations always subtract from your happiness.

When you stop taking things personally, you will be happier.

Anytime you're angry, look in the mirror and ask the hard question: what's really bothering me?

Sustaining happiness, regardless of the circumstances, is the greatest accomplishment.

Spend five minutes a day with your eyes closed, sitting alone, breathing deeply—and your life will change.

Freedom is the ability to make a choice between misery and happiness.

Happiness is being at peace with whatever happens and whatever doesn't happen.

When your personal vibration is connected to the Universe, you are going to dominate all other vibrations that you encounter. When you live connected, happiness is the result.

My happiness depends solely on me and the countless choices I make throughout every moment of every day.

Guess what? You learned how to feel bad. That means you can learn how to feel good.

You will receive a match to your vibration. Whatever you cause, you will experience the effect. I repeat, whatever you cause you will experience the effect.

Anyone can be happy when the sun is shining. I want to know who you are when the sun isn't out.

What does "being happy" really mean? It means that I am at peace with whatever happens AND

I am at peace with whatever doesn't happen.

All labels subtract from Happiness.

Everything that happens is a response to how you feel. That's why my number-one priority is Happiness.

Can you compare the stars in the sky? When you compare yourself to others, get ready to be unhappy. All comparisons subtract from happiness.

When you attach to an outcome, you subtract from your Happiness. All attachments subtract from Happiness. No exceptions.

Some people want predictions for their future. I say this: I can't predict the future, but I can predict that whatever happens to you is in perfect order. And I can also predict that whatever happens to you will be for your betterment.

CHAPTER 15

Conclusion
Life Is a Gift

Close your eyes and think back: Can you remember being blown away by a gift you received? It does not matter who gave it to you, just think about what that gift was. I'll wait.

Maybe, if you are fortunate, you can think of more than one gift that left you speechless—that gift that physically caused your eyebrows to rise while your mouth fell open in appreciation. You might have physically jumped up and down, unable to contain your joy. Do you remember how happy you were? Can you remember how you felt?

I am here to announce that your LIFE is such a gift! In fact, the gift of LIFE is more valuable than any other gift given to you or that can ever be given to you. To be able to experience this thing we call LIFE, in any form or fashion, is a daily gift. It is beyond words and explanation. With every breath we take, we are experiencing Life.

When you wake up each morning, take a brief moment to say "Thank you." The Universe does not require us to be thankful. However, the Universe will *match* your vibration of gratitude with more to be grateful for. As your day unfolds, remember how fortunate you are to have this gift of Life. How do *you* choose to live it?

ABOUT THE AUTHOR

Rebecca L. Norrington is first and foremost a student of the Universe and ITs Laws. She has a Bachelor of Science degree in Psychology, along with decades of education and training on topics from Spirituality to Human Behavior. Her professional journey includes several vocations: Happiness Specialist, Radio & TV Personality, Intuitive, Healer, Author, Speaker, Teacher, and Fitness Instructor.

In August 2011, Rebecca premiered *RealitySpirituality*, an online radio show that shares revolutionary tools and strategies that enable you to sustain a personal vibration of internal peace and contentment, regardless of your external circumstances. Rebecca loves to focus on everyday circumstances and events and how these circumstances and events align with our personal vibration. Rebecca's *RealitySpirituality* audience has grown rapidly and currently has millions of listeners around the world. Rebecca has a clear vision of hosting *RealitySpirituality* on a major network channel. *RealitySpirituality* can be heard LIVE every Saturday and Sunday 7:00 A.M. (PST).

For more information visit: www.rebeccanorrington.com & www.realityspirituality.com.

Services: Intuitive, Healer, Radio Host, Author, Speaker, Health and Fitness Instructor

Career Focus: Television, Radio, Speaker, Seminars, Workshops, Spiritual Entertainer, Travel

Rebecca has been an AFAA (Aerobics and Fitness Association of America) certified Aerobic Instructor and Personal Trainer since 1982. During her 30+ years in the fitness industry, she has taught BootCamp, Cycling, High/Low Impact, Step, Weight Training and Conditioning, Aqua Aerobics, Silver Splash, Senior Fitness, and Basic Stretch. Rebecca also created two specialty classes: AquaBootCamp and Facersize.

1982 – Present
Fitness Instructor

1985 – Present
Mother

1992 – 2003
Amateur Talent Show Producer & Director

2005
Private/Corporate Event Planner, Writer

2008

Toastmaster; Facilitated two Happiness Seminars: *It's All about You* and *You Are the Answer*

2009

Toastmaster Divisional Contest Winner in Inspirational and Humorous Speech categories

December 26, 2010 – February 6, 2011

Began a 40-day vow of silence while attending Agape's New Year's Meditation Retreat facilitated by Rev. Michael Bernard Beckwith. "I learned the power of using energy, instead of words, to communicate with others."

2011 – Present

Created *RealitySpirituality* Radio Show, Author, Speaker, and Healer

2013

One of seventeen contributing Authors to *If I Knew Then What I Know Now, Our Quest for Quality or Life;* Radio Guest and Host

Authors That Changed My Life

Ernest Holmes, Abraham-Hicks, M. Scott Peck, Deepak Chopra, Eckhart Tolle

Family

Ralph & Marcelle Norrington
Nathan M. Norrington
Ccid E. Cartwright
Anne Cartwright
Cidney Cartwright
Joyce Shafer

AUTHOR'S NOTE

It's a challenge to construct "who I am," when I'm continually changing both spiritually and personally with every passing day. Who I am *today* is *not* who I will be tomorrow. Sharing the events of my life based on what I've accomplished is a small piece to an *on-growing* puzzle. Every event and every person in my life has significantly influenced me; and each day is a welcomed adventure to grow even more. The one constant in my Life is my commitment to spiritual and personal growth. This commitment has brought me increasing amounts of inner peace, contentment, and Happiness. My purpose and ultimate destiny is to share, with fun and humor, the strategies, tools, and lessons I've learned with as many as will listen. *~rln*